The Diary of Sarah Tabitha Reid, 1868-1873

The Diary of Sarah Tabitha Reid, 1868-1873

EDITED WITH AN INTRODUCTION
BY DELIGHT W. DODYK

Published by the
MONMOUTH COUNTY HISTORICAL ASSOCIATION
FREEHOLD, NEW JERSEY
2001

PUBLISHED WITH SUPPORT FROM THE

New Jersey Historical Commission

ISBN 0-9705560-0-4
Designed by Suzanne G. Bennett
Printed by The Riverview Press, Little Silver, New Jersey
Printed on acid-free paper in the United States of America

Published by Monmouth County Historical Association
70 Court Street, Freehold, New Jersey 07728
FIRST EDITION

Editor's Acknowledgements

I am indebted to the many friends and colleagues who helped in the detective work of deciphering aspects of Sarah Reid's diary. Lee Ellen Griffith, Director of the Monmouth County Historical Association, introduced me to the world of Sarah Reid by leisurely drives through the Freehold area identifying places associated with the Reids. Carla Z. Tobias, Librarian/Archivist of the Monmouth County Historical Association, was always ready to guide me in the wealth of newspapers, maps, and other local historical material available in the MCHA collections. Bernadette M. Rogoff, Curator of the Monmouth County Historical Association, whose creativity and imagination brought Sarah Reid's diary to life through a museum exhibition, shared her insights and research. MCHA volunteer Jean Houston first transcribed the diary to get the project started, and volunteer Cheryl Wolf surveyed newspapers of the period to add to our knowledge of Sarah Reid's world. The photography for this volume was expertly done by volunteer George Fox.

William Harris, Archivist of the Princeton Theological Seminary, gave me invaluable help in identifying the various Presbyterian clergy and missionaries mentioned by Sarah Reid and aided me in identifying various hymns. Alice Copeland of the Drew University Library proved to be a skilled sleuth in the world of Presbyterian hymnology; she introducing me to the 19th century singing school tradition and to the extensive hymn book collection at the Drew Library. Kate Skrebutenas of the Speer Library at the Princeton Theological Seminary helped locate the newspapers Sarah read. Donald Kent, M.D. of the Drew University graduate faculty and Francis P. Chinard, M.D. of the University of Medicine and Dentistry of New Jersey gave helpful insights into the puzzling medical aspects of the diary. Lois Densky-Wolfe, Director of the History of Medicine Collection at the Smith Library of the University of Medicine and Dentistry of New Jersey provided biographical information on various doctors mentioned in the diary. Genealogist Eileen Jourdan Thompson was generous with her genealogical research on Sarah Reid's family and answered questions about the convoluted family interrelationships. Robert MacAvoy and Paul Schoop drew my attention to the full story of the tragic Sunday School drownings mentioned in the diary. Suzanne Bennett has sensitively and artfully designed this book and her work is enhanced by the fine quality of Riverview Press' printing. Scholars will appreciate the detailed index done by Nick Humez.

Dr. Carolyn DeSwarte Gifford of Evanston, IL nurtured my progress in the process of diary editing; and Dr. Nancy R. Jaicks of Ridgewood, NJ was a careful and critical reader. Various writers for the Women's Project of New Jersey Inc. helped to pave the way for understanding Sarah's diary by the research they have done on other New Jersey women diarists, whose journals have been preserved in archives around the state.

DELIGHT WING DODYK
Drew University

FOREWORD

In 1993, the Monmouth County Historical Association was contacted by Dr. and Mrs. Charles B. Ashanin of Indianapolis regarding an old leather-bound diary that they had inherited. The volume turned out to be a treasure – a woman's journal revealing a wealth of information about everyday life on a Freehold farm in the years following the Civil War. Sarah Reid wrote about the rewards and hardships of farm and family life, about the comfort she found through her faith in God, and about the world she saw around her.

The intimate, immediate quality of her writing charmed and inspired us all. Former Librarian Barbara Carver Smith began research on the Reid family. Curator Bernadette Rogoff developed an exhibition featuring passages from the diary brought to life with objects from the museum collections arranged in tableaus to reflect Sarah's world as she described it. We were very fortunate to work with Dr. Delight W. Dodyk who brought her considerable expertise in the field of women's history to the project. Her thoughtful editing and annotation of the diary and her thoroughly researched monograph perfectly compliment the spirit of the original document. Mary R. Murrin of the New Jersey Historical Commission offered enthusiasm, encouragement and guidance.

A series of three generous grants from the New Jersey Historical Commission made it possible to publish this book and to bring Sarah's journal to life through the museum exhibition, "The World of Sarah Tabitha Reid," which was on view from July 1997 to June 1998. The exhibition received an award of commendation from the American Association for State and Local History. Our sincere thanks also go to the following individuals who made contributions toward the publication of this journal: Ellen Adams, Pearl and John Anderson, Margaret Folgore, Mary Z. Ginn, Rebecca L. Griffith, James F. Higgins, Tabitha Huber, Frederick C. Kniesler Jr., Charles C. Martin, Mary McKeown, Joanne Mullen, Marion D. Noren, Robert I. Owen, Judith H. Stanley, Mary Lou Strong, Bonnie Torcivia, and Jane R. Zdancewic.

LEE ELLEN GRIFFITH
Director
Monmouth County
Historical Association

Sarah Tabitha Reid's Diary, 1868-1873

A very stormy morning. Snowed all day. I had a bad head ache all day. Willie is assleep on my lap. I can not write. Elwood & Leonard went away in the evening.

[Sunday, February 12, 1871]

A dull morning. Becky washed and worked very smart. I sewed some and Ironed some. Busy all day. Wet my flowers by moon light and set out one flower in my mound. It is a splendid night. The catydids are singing and the children is sitting out doors telling stories and I am writing with a musketoe around my ears bussing and biting by turns, and now I am going to read some in my bible and have prayers and go to bed, and such a kind heavenly father to take care of me and all my dear ones where ever they are. Such an all seeing God what would we do without his watchful care and all with such a tender hand. I feel as if no evil could come where Gods eye was and I know it is every where beholding the evil and the good.

[Tuesday, August 9, 1870]

As Sarah Reid sat with her visiting grandson on her lap, she managed to write down what she felt were the basic events of her day, not in the privacy of a boudoir, but in the midst of her family on a snowy Sabbath in her West Freehold farm house. On this day she took what precious time she could to jot down the bare essentials of her daily record. At other times she wrote her entries after the fact, at a later time after a busy week, when she looked back and reconstructed her days to keep the record up to date. Sometimes she was able to spare the time to be more reflective and to indulge a creative impulse, sitting in her door yard on a balmy August evening. Sarah's diary is a form of autobiography, a form of self-representation. Unlike narrative autobiography which requires consistency of representation and style, her diary is of the moment, recording the day-to-day without needing to suggest continuity. A diary is a form eminently suited to women like Sarah Reid whose work and daily lives are often marked by repetition and incessant interruptions.

Sarah's diary is in some ways what one student of women's diaries calls a "truly private diary," one of the "bare-bones works" written primarily to record the weather, "visits to and from neighbors, or public occurrences of both the institutional and the sensational sort." Such diaries are written "with neither art nor artifice, they are so terse they seem coded; no reader outside the author's immediate society or household could understand them without extra-textual information."[1] This characterization fits Sarah's diary, but only to a certain extent; her diary, like other "truly private diaries," needs contextualization and annotation. Yet Sarah's diary is not consistently "bare-bones." While she writes without self-conscious style or apparent design, Sarah reveals and expresses herself through her diary. She reflects on her family, on her situation, and especially on her interior religious life, using her diary as a sympathetic confidante to complain to and rejoice with. We do not know where Sarah got the idea of keeping a diary and what her models were. Perhaps other women in her family or in her circle of friends kept diaries. Perhaps her devotional reading led her to some of the Protestant religious journals that were published as devotional guides. Sarah's diary contains elements of a daily record, of an interior monologue, as well as a religious journal in which she contemplated her relationship to her God. It provides us with more than daily data by revealing the aspirations and spiritual life of this Monmouth County farm woman.

Why did Sarah Tabitha Reid keep a diary when she did? Is the diary now deposited in the archives of the Monmouth County Historical Association her complete journal, or were there other volumes that have been lost? Sarah gives no overt clues in her diary. Certainly, given the long days of hard work that filled her life, keeping a diary took considerable initiative and motivation. According to one authority on American diaries, "The life of a diary is often born of a tension, a disequilibrium in the life of its author, which needs to be resolved or held in check."[2] It seems likely that Sarah started her diary because she was at a special period in her life, a period of tension. She was just short of her 50th birthday, a relatively advanced age at a time when life expectancy for white women was around 61 years. Her family's life pattern was changing in ways that deeply affected her personally. She was living in a time of economic and social transition after the Civil War, and her own family was experiencing dramatic changes in its economic and social configuration. Sarah's diary allowed her to record her daily activities, while expressing her feelings, both positive and negative, about what was happening to herself, her husband, and her children. Implicit in a diary is a sense of personal history.

Who is the intended reader of this diary? Was it intended only for Sarah's eyes? Sarah's family must have known she was keeping a diary. She kept it openly, and she must have been aware that the temptation would be great for her family, her young daughters especially, to peek into it. Perhaps they succumbed, with or without permission. Perhaps Sarah's more reflective entries were unspoken messages to

---

[1] Lynn Z. Bloom, "'I Write for Myself and Strangers: Private Diaries as Public Documents," in Suzanne L. Bunkers and Cynthia A. Huff, *Inscribing the Daily: Critical Essays on Women's Diaries* (Amherst: University of Massachusetts Press, 1996), p. 25. Bloom uses as an example of a "truly private diary" the diary of Martha Ballard, a late-eighteenth century Maine midwife brilliantly edited by Laurel T. Ulrich in *The Midwife's Tale: The Life of Martha Ballard, Based on Her Diary, 1785-1812* (New York: Knopf, 1990).

[2] Steven E. Kagle, *American Diary Literature* (Boston: Twayne Publishers, 1979), p. 17.

her family meant to reveal herself or to instruct. Yet she probably never dreamed that we, as readers 130 years later, would examine her record as a valuable document of New Jersey women's past. We have the unforeseen privilege of being admitted to one woman's self-representation, the privilege of viewing her world as she saw it in a specific time and place. We may read this diary from different perspectives: for insights into women's social history, for psychological insights, for medical information, for religious history, for local cultural, agricultural, and historical information, for linguistic purposes, or from a sociological perspective. Diaries lend themselves to such interdisciplinary critiques, and as historical and literary documents, are multifaceted. Every diary has special insights to offer.

We know only a little about Sarah Tabitha (Appleton) Reid's life. She was born in Freehold Township on November 30, 1818. Her parents, Sarah Lawrence (Reid) and Abijah Appleton both died when she was a small child, her mother in 1820 and her father in 1821.[3] She and her younger brother, James, were raised by their grandparents Margaret (Laird) and Joseph Reid, and Sarah remained very close to her mother's younger sisters, Harriet, Margaret, and Susan. We do not know exactly where she grew up or what her early years were like. Her grandmother and her aunts were members of the Old Tennent Presbyterian Church so it is certain she was raised in the Old Tennent congregation.[4] She was a devout member of the Old Tennent Church at the time she kept her diary. Judging by Sarah's handwriting, grammar, and spelling, she had a rudimentary education, learning to read, write and do simple arithmetic as a child. As an adult she loved to read and was largely self-taught. Most of her reading was religious literature, the formal language of which deeply infused her vocabulary and spiritual expression.

Sarah married William Henry Reid (1817-1894) on December 30, 1840 when she was 22 and he was 23. Sarah and William were both descendents, she through her mother and he through his father, of James Reid, who immigrated from Scotland between 1680 and 1686 and was an original settler in Manalapan. William's was a large extended family. He was one of eleven children of Hannah (Miller) and John Reid of Manalapan, and his family was part of the active network of kin that appears and reappears in Sarah's diary.[5] William began acquiring farm land in 1840 before he was married, and over the years the couple acquired more

[3] Genealogical information for Sarah Reid's family has been prepared by genealogist Eileen Jourdan Thompson of Hazlet; also see Frank R. Symmes, *History of the Old Tennent Church* (Cranbury, NJ: George W. Burroughs, 1902), p. 432.

[4] Symmes, *History of the Old Tennent Church*, pp. 90, 193.

[5] Genealogical information for William Reid's family has been prepared by genealogist Eileen Jourdan Thompson of Hazlet; also see Symmes, *History of the Old Tennent Church*, pp. 433-34.

Family Members Mentioned in Sarah's Diary

Margaret Laird (1770-1857)   m. 1788   Joseph Reid (1768-)

Four Other Children

Harriet (1802-) m. John Reid Jewell

Susan (-) m. Gilbert Applegate

Margaret (1807-1893) m. Benjamin Van Cleve

John Reid (1789-1868) Ten Other Children

Hannah Miller (1792-)

Abijah Appleton (-1821)

Sarah L. Reid (-1820) m. 17 Jan. 1818

Sarah Tabitha Appleton (30 Nov. 1818-16 Mar. 1888)

William Henry Reid (15 Oct. 1817-29 Aug. 1894)

m. 30 Dec. 1840

Sarah Elizabeth (26 Sept. 1841 -15 Jan. 1853)

Hannah Matilda (16 Sept. 1845 -14 May 1930)

Benjamin Conover Preston 24 Dec. 1863

m.

William Elwood Tennent (1 Nov. 1849 -24 Feb. 1916)

Margaret Elizabeth (19 Oct. 1857 -22 Jul. 1916)

Florence Augusta (20 Feb.1860- 20 Feb. 1934)

Sarah Frances (2 Dec. 1864-1931)

Cora Elizabeth (25 Mar. 1867-1950)

Joseph Henry (7 Jan. 1869-1931)

William Elwood (7 Jan. 1869-1889)

Viola Virginia (5 Feb. 1871-1904)

Three Other Children Not Mentioned in the Diary

land from David R. and Mary Ann Reid, distant relatives.[6] William was listed as a farmer in the 1860 United States census but at some point after that became a bricklayer by trade.[7]

Sarah and William struggled financially. When his father died in 1868, William received a small inheritance that was unequal to that of his brothers. It was around this time that Sarah began her diary. As she confided on October 4 1869:

> Oh it is so hard to see him go from home to keep his family when his Father had plenty to make all of his children comfortable to get along in the world if he had divided it equally among them but some of them he has left more than they will ever need.

And again on August 4, 1870 she wrote:

> If his father could see from the land of rest where I hope he has gone what his injustice has done to make some sons rich and crush some down with no help which he was so able to give and never would have felt it. All the wagon he ever gave him when he went to farming was worn out when he gave it to him. He gave four of his sons farms and gave him but two thousand altogether cattle and all the same that he gave his girls.[8]

During the span of the diary, William was working and living in New York City for lengthy periods, between March and December, to support his family, commuting back and forth occasionally to help with farm tasks.

Sarah and William had five children, four of whom lived to adulthood. Sarah Elizabeth, the eldest, was born in 1841 nine months after their marriage, but died in January 1853 just after her twelfth birthday. Hannah Matilda (Tillie) was born in 1845 and William Elwood Tennent (Elwood or El) was born in 1848. Margaret Elizabeth (Lizzie) was born in 1857, followed in 1862 by Florence Augusta (Flora or sometimes Gussie). Whether Sarah had other pregnancies ending in miscarriage or stillbirth we do not know. She was just a little over 44 years old when her last child was born.

Sarah Reid's diary, kept between the autumn of 1868 and the end of 1871, gives us a rare insight into the daily routine and relationships of a farm family living at a time when New Jersey was rapidly industrializing and urbanizing, and when

---

[6] This acreage became encumbered with mortgage and was sold by Sarah and William in 1878 to Levi S. Bond. [Deed of Sale, December 18, 1878]

[7] William Reid was listed as a farmer in the 1860 U. S. Census and a bricklayer in 1880. The Reids were not enumerated in the 1870 census.

[8] Land records show that William's brothers purchased land from their father.

the farm communities closer to urban areas were growing and developing.[9] The Reids were, in many ways, typical of the farming families of the area. Modestly educated, self-sufficient but giving and receiving neighborly help, well-acquainted in the area but not distinguished by public leadership or notoriety, they were ordinary folks. They were hard working people whose lives were structured by the cycles of the growing season and the demands of William's trade. The entire family, even the youngest child, was involved in the working of the farm and household. However, in one very important way, the Reids differed from their neighbors. While Sarah's life was fully bounded by her responsibilities as a farm wife, William was a seasonal commuter, splitting his time between the farm and his work in what we assume was bricklaying, in New York City.

The location of the Reid family farm made William's work pattern possible. Located just a few miles southwest of Freehold, close to the main road from Freehold to Mount Holly (now Route 537), the farm was in the midst of Monmouth County farm country. Much of the local farm land had been nearly depleted in the early nineteenth century until the English technique of applying local, nutrient-rich marl to the soil was introduced, and farming in Monmouth County experienced renewed vitality.[10] The Monmouth seashore was the first part of the New Jersey coast to develop as a popular summer resort area, and the hotels there touted the benefits of fresh, healthful produce from local New Jersey farms.[11] In 1853, when the Freehold & Jamesburg Agricultural Railroad connected to the Camden and Amboy Railroad (built to connect the Delaware River near Philadelphia with the Raritan Bay), local farmers achieved improved access by rail and ferry to major urban markets for farm produce and crops. The railroad also opened the area to increased commercial development, introduced a growing immigrant labor force, and connected local workers, like William Reid, to new job markets. The Reids were near enough to Freehold, the county seat, for the family to take advantage of the commercial opportunities and resources there. Living within a reasonable proximity to the railroad, the family had access to New York City as well as Trenton. Theirs was a rural life that was becoming less remote and more complex.

We first meet Sarah and her family when her diary entries begin in November 1868. She was almost 50 and William (whom she refers to as Mr. Reid) was 51. Sarah's intimate private household was relatively small. Tillie, Sarah's eldest child, then 23 years of age, was not living at home, having been married for nearly five

---

[9] In 1870, 43.7% of New Jersey's population of 906,000 were defined as urban dwellers.

[10] Hubert G. Schmidt, *Agriculture in New Jersey: A Three-Hundred-Year History* (New Brunswick: Rutgers University Press, 1973), p. 129. For contemporary sources on the agricultural uses of marl see also, Horace Greeley, *What I Know of Farming: A Series of Brief and Plain Expositions* (New York: G. W. Carleton & Co., 1871), pp. 109, 142, 166-167, and *Monmouth Democrat*, June 17, 1841 and June 27, 1867.

[11] Anne Bishop and Doris Simpson, *The Victorian Seaside Cookbook* (Newark: New Jersey Historical Society, 1983), p. 2.

years to Benjamin Conover Preston, known as Con. They had been married at Sarah and William's home by the family minister, Rev. Archibald Cobb, the pastor of the Old Tennent Church. When Sarah began her diary, Tillie and Con had two children, four-year-old Fannie and a toddler, 1 1/2 year-old Lizzie, but over the course of the diary Tillie bore twin boys, Joe and Willie, in 1869 and then in 1871 another daughter, Viola. They lived quite a distance away, probably in Englishtown, about a two-hour buggy ride from the family farm. Elwood, Sarah and William's only son, was 19. He lived at home helping with the farm, but also enjoyed some independence and a social life of his own outside the family. In 1870 he attended the Freehold Institute, a secondary school for boys run by the Rev. A. G. Chambers. He decided against farming as a life work and in March 1870 took a job in Freehold as a clerk in the D. C. Perrine dry goods store. Sarah feared his working in town, thinking he would "learn bad ways, or ingure (sic) his health."[12] Tillie and Con wanted Sarah and William to let them take on the family farm at the time, but Sarah was reluctant to move. She mentions this issue just once and very tersely in her diary. Elwood continued to live at home part of the time and to help out on the farm.[13]

The two younger girls also lived at home. Lizzie, 11 years old at the diary's start, was a difficult child for Sarah, quick to sass and challenge her mother's authority and bent on having her own way. She shouldered a good deal of the housework and was increasingly a mainstay for her mother, albeit unwillingly at times. During the course of the diary, Lizzie celebrated her important twelfth birthday and was allowed to drive the carriage by herself. (To Sarah's dismay, she tended to drive very fast.) Florence was 6 1/2 and not much older than Sarah's granddaughter, Fannie, when Sarah's diary begins. Despite her age she was an important hand around the house and barn yard and more companionable than her older sister. By the time she was nine she was baking cakes, doing laundry, and assuming a substantial load of the household work. The girls attended the local school intermittently. Compulsory education was not mandated in New Jersey until 1875, so the girls could go and come as the family needed.

The work of the family followed a rough division of labor, defined more by physical ability and traditional skills than by the niceties of gender-defined "separate spheres." William, Elwood, and seasonal hired hands performed the heavy farm work of plowing, planting crops and the kitchen garden, harvesting, and managing the larger farm stock. In the winter they did the butchering of the larger animals, hauled marl for fertilizer, chopped wood, carted hay, and hauled ice from a nearby pond. William bought, sold, and traded their carriage and work horses. The men occasionally helped with household tasks such as churning and candle making, and even the cooking.

---

[12] Entry February 28, 1870.
[13] See entries for February 28 and March 11, 1870.

Charles McDonald (husband of
Lizzie Reid McDonald, son-in-law of
Sarah Tabitha Reid). Monmouth County
Historical Association Library & Archives

Lizzie Reid McDonald (daughter of
Sarah Tabitha Reid, wife of Charles
McDonald), later in life. Monmouth County
Historical Association Library & Archives

Sarah's work, and the work of her hired female help, also involved heavy physical labor, especially onerous for Sarah as she entered her fifties. In reality, Sarah bore the major burden of the farm, with William away for prolonged periods of time. She increasingly experienced the pains of rheumatism and other ill-defined ailments, the result of years of toil. She relied heavily on her son and young daughters, and on occasional hired girls and women to get the necessary tasks done. Her young daughters, especially Lizzie, frequently performed the work of grown women. Baking, cleaning, ironing, and laundering all fell into Sarah's domain. She barely mentions the daily routine work in her diary: the morning and evening feeding of farm animals and poultry, milking cows, collecting eggs, and hauling water and firewood for household use. Many of these chores were probably performed by Lizzie and Florence. She tells more about the seasonal farm tasks such as butchering, setting of poultry, searching for wandering livestock, harvesting strawberries. She records, for her own personal satisfaction and validation, the more skilled household tasks of baking cakes, breads, and pies, laundering and ironing, cleaning, sewing and mending the family clothing, preparing meals for visitors and farm hands, and the seasonal household projects of stove blacking and whitewashing, candle making, and even wall papering.

Sarah's economic contributions to her family were substantial. Her unpaid labor as cook and housekeeper was taken for granted by herself and her family. Like many farm wives, she earned cash through the sale of butter, cream, eggs, tallow, and poultry that she took to town or sold to people on order. Her earnings were not enumerated on the census, indeed they were legally William's under New Jersey law, and Sarah did not consider them hers. On at least one occasion she regretted the fact she had no discretionary money of her own to donate to foreign missionaries. The pennies she gave to foreign missions were painstakingly saved by giving up sugar with her tea. She had enough cash, however, to hire local girls and women to help her with the heavier housework: the laundry, ironing and heavy cleaning. Elmira, a young single woman possibly the daughter of neighbors, the Gravatts, Mrs. Mack, an Irish neighbor, Rebecca, another young helper, and other paid helpers aided Sarah. Inside the front cover of her diary, Sarah kept a tally of the work performed by Elmira and the money owed her. These hired women were occasional extra hands, not servants; they often lived with the Reids and shared in the family activities.[14] When hired help was unavailable, Sarah and the girls struggled to keep ahead of the housework themselves.

The Reids raised most of their food themselves. They kept a kitchen garden that yielded potatoes, peas, beets, onions, beans, tomatoes, summer savory, and other vegetables. They raised strawberries for table and market, and had access to pears, quinces, gooseberries, apples, cranberries, cherries, and peaches to eat fresh or to preserve. Huckleberries and nuts they gathered wild. They raised their own chickens, ducks and turkeys and sent some to market. Their cows provided them with milk and cream, and they made their own butter and ice cream. They butchered their beef and hogs for their use and for market, making their own sausage, lard, and tallow. Grain crops of oats, corn and wheat provided feed for their animals and flour that was milled for them by local millers. Sarah did the baking of breads, pies, cakes, and other baked goods. Though we know she must have bought staples at the local stores, fish was the only food Sarah mentions purchasing, and that from a peddler.

We must speculate about the configuration of Sarah's home, for her diary entries are more task-oriented that visually descriptive. The house had a kitchen,

[14] The diary of Abbie Eliza Magee of Marlboro, though written some 45 years after Sarah Reid's, is relevant here because it illumines the life of a Monmouth County woman, who, like Sarah's helpers, worked in the homes of other women for pay. Magee kept a diary during 1905 when she was in her late 50s. Magee was single and supported herself by living and working in the homes of friends and relatives; she did housework, helped with cooking and preserving, laundering and ironing, and particularly sewing. Magee was a member of the Old Tennent Church, and though thirty years younger than Sarah, may well have been acquainted with her. Her short diary reveals a work style and community relationships very like those of the women whom Sarah paid to help her with her housework. [See Abbie Eliza Magee, Diary, Special Collections/University Archives, Alexander Library, Rutgers University; Magee is profiled in Joan N. Burstyn, *Past and Promise: Lives of New Jersey Women* (Syracuse: Syracuse University Press, 1997), pp. 169-170]

sitting room or parlor, pantries, and several bedrooms, and a cellar, but we do not know what her house looked like, inside or out, nor, in any detail, what equipment she used to do her housework. House technology, in general, was developing rapidly at the time; some well-to-do homes were being built with central heating and cold running water, even with indoor toilets. Iron cooking stoves had long ago replaced open-hearth cooking except in the most primitive homes, while iron heating stoves were used instead of fireplaces to heat main rooms. Gas lighting replaced oil and candles for lighting, and improved cooking utensils such as the simple manual egg beater lightened the work of housewives to a certain extent. The introduction of the treadle-operated sewing machine dramatically transformed the sewing tasks of women. Some of this changing technology was present in the Reid's home even though such household innovations tended to reach rural areas and modest homes much later than more comfortable urban households.[15] Sarah had a wood stove for cooking and baking. The house was apparently heated by cast iron stoves, with a coal stove in the sitting room. Though Sarah and William made candles with tallow from their beef, they probably did not rely solely on them for lighting. The family used wash basins in the bedrooms for personal washing, supplied presumably by well water, though Sarah never actually mentions a well. We do know Sarah had a treadle sewing machine. She, with the help of Lizzie, Florence, and this wonderful machine, sewed most of the clothing for herself and the girls, William's and Elwood's lighter apparel, quilts and comforters, and rags for rugs that were probably woven by a carpet weaver in Freehold.

Sarah benefited from being near a large metropolitan area and close to stores in the villages of West Freehold, Freehold, Manalapan, Englishtown, and even New Brunswick. She shopped in these towns for yard goods, notions, and household goods. Nearby there was a telegraph office she could use when she was anxious about William in New York City. Though the family drove their own horses and carriage for transportation, going as far afield as New Brunswick and Long Branch on occasion, they also had good rail service nearby. William took the "cars" to the city, they sent produce to market in New York via rail, and the family made an excursion to the September fair in Trenton by train. Most important, ready access to New York City enabled William to work for an essential cash income.

Proximity to Freehold, the county seat, also made medical attention more available to the family. Nursing the family when they were ailing was generally Sarah's work. She climbed numerous flights of stairs caring for the bed-ridden and used a rudimentary store of concoctions and techniques when family members were sick or injured. She made mustard plasters, applied Wells liniment, used onion cloths, and prepared foot soakings. Nevertheless, doctors were also available to

---

[15] For more information about the development of household technology see Susan Strasser, *Never Done: A History of American Housework* (New York: Pantheon, 1983) and Ruth Schwartz Cowan, *More Work For Mother: The Ironies of Household Technology from the Open Hearth to the Microwave* (New York: Basic Books, 1983).

make house calls in emergencies. Such was the case when William came home from New York with a severe gastro-intestinal condition and when Florence developed an alarmingly high fever. In a rare preventive precaution, both the girls were vaccinated for smallpox by the doctor in December 1871. In general, however, the family simply lived through their various colds and flu-like complaints, with Sarah attempting to alleviate symptoms. Sarah worried, understandably, about typhoid, scarlet fever, and heat stroke, and fretted about her family's health. Her worry did not keep her from visiting relatives with typhoid fever, but she was especially wary of the itinerants and vagrants that were sheltered from time to time on the farm, fearing the possibility of contagion. As her own health deteriorated over the course of her diary, we perceive the limits of medical knowledge and care at the time. Whether from exhaustion, stress, menopause, or from some major, undiagnosed condition, she was plagued by frequent headaches, rheumatism, and other muscular or neurological pain. Her ability to do her housework was hampered, and she relied more and more heavily on her daughters, other relatives, and paid help to assist her.[16]

Sarah's diary reveals some of the interpersonal stresses of the Reids' lives that seem remarkably familiar to the modern world. Money was a worry, as was William's work away from home. With William working in New York City during the busiest months of the farming cycle, Sarah's work load increased along with her loneliness. She experienced what many modern wives do when husbands are absent for prolonged periods. She felt lonely and afraid during his extended absences and bemoaned his needing to work so hard to support the family; but she also felt resentful of the situation they were in. Sarah consoled herself with the income William made, commenting on October 25, 1870, "I had a wakeful night. Had a letter from my husband. Was so glad to hear from him. He is making six dollars a day but we do need him so much at home this time of year."[17]

While William was away, major responsibility lay with Sarah, but when he returned to the household, she had to adjust to his reasserted authority. A minor family controversy on February 27, 1870 suggests the tensions Sarah felt when William reassumed his patriarchal role. She wrote:

> Was part ready for church when Mr. Reid began to hurry me as he always does. When I said I would stay home but Flora and Lizzie was so disapoint-

---

[16] I have searched Sarah's diary in vain for clues as to whether she was going through menopause, which she may well have completed by the time of her diary. Her diary in general is devoid of any mention of bodily functions, except when family members were ill. Diary editors have sometimes found in women's diaries notations or codes indicating that women were keeping records of menstruation, presumably with the idea of controlling child bearing. See Janet Farrell Brodie, *Contraception and Abortion in 19th Century America* (Ithaca: Cornell University Press, 1994), pp. 9-37.

[17] William was earning considerably more than the average American bricklayer whose daily wage was reported to be $3.45. In 1869, 1870, and 1871, William worked approximately 7 months of each year in New York. If he worked six days a week, he would have worked 168 days, earning $1008.

ed I concluded to go and Mr. Reid said we should not go. I felt very much
provoked but said nothing. It is too bad for men to controll their wives in
every thing and they are so nice before marriage. No one thinks they are
always to give up their wishes to pleas those that are no better than they
are. I have always been so fond of pease I would bear any thing for pease,
but any one must keep on bearing.

Sarah thus speaks directly of the acquiescence to male authority expected of
the nineteenth-century wife, revealing as she does the resentments such acquies-
ence created, especially for a mature woman carrying so significant a portion of the
family burdens.

In her treatment of her son, Sarah nevertheless perpetuated into the next gen-
eration patterns of female subordination. Elwood, as the proxy head of household
in William's absence, was given his way when he chose to use the horse and buggy
or when his plans conflicted with Sarah's or the girls. He was allowed to come in at
all hours of the night, and Sarah prepared meals for him regardless of the time.
Sarah, however, tended to see his behavior as that of an ungrateful child, rather
than as the assumption of male prerogatives. "I have always been willing to sucrifice any thing almost for his enjoyment with the greatest pleasure, and never have
an unpleasant thought about it. That is the difference in a mothers love & a
childs," she wrote on November 27, 1870.

Many of the stresses Sarah experienced were psychological as well as physical.
This was especially the case when she and Lizzie were in conflict. Lizzie's temper
tantrums and verbal outbursts were extremely upsetting to Sarah, who not infrequently developed headaches or rheumatism pain afterward. In one such incident
on November 30, 1870 Lizzie and Sarah argued about the cost of singing school.
"She went on all day like a tyrant," wrote Sarah.

All the impudince she could think of and every thing she could say to try
me. I was tempted to get a whip and give her some of it but I knew a little
would not do and I was two busy to spend a long time batling with her.

That night Sarah was wracked with so much pain that relatives and the doctor were called in to help. Sarah was sympathetic to the fact that her children did
a great deal of work in the house and farm. "Florrence is doing the night work out
doors. It is too bad for a little girl to milk and feed hogs and wood and every thing,"
she wrote on October 29, 1870. But she wanted the girls' obedience and the emotional support of willing workers as she increasingly needed their help. In general,
she took a tolerant or at least non-confrontational stance toward their behavior,
for better or for worse. Household peace seems to have been her overarching
desire.

Sarah's relationship with her married daughter was, of necessity, somewhat more distant. The two families visited back and forth, with the whole family coming to stay overnight or several days. Sarah and William enjoyed their grandchildren and helped out by having the children come to stay for prolonged periods. Sarah was called upon to help in emergencies, as was her son-in-law's mother. Sarah worried about Tillie, with her several very young children and a household to maintain. On March 29, 1870 she wrote:

> Mr Reid took us all to see Tillie and my heart was sick to see her. She is worked until she is nothing but a frame and a very slender one at that. Her four little ones is two much for one to wait on and all the rest she has to do, and has so little rest at night. If I get a little smarter I will take Fannie and Willie if she will let them come. Came home in the evening and could not sleep until nearly morning worrying about Tillie. I am affraid she will not live through the spring. I thought of every way and every thing to save her life. I can think of nothing but to get her something to strengthen her.

When Tillie's fifth baby was born the next February, two of the children stayed with Sarah and William for several weeks, but Sarah did not attend the birthing or even see the new granddaughter until she was several days old. Well she might have been critical of yet another baby so soon. Modern scholarship has demonstrated that contraceptive information was generally available at this time. A plethora of self-help literature emerged after 1850, and newspapers and magazines carried ads for various devices and techniques usually couched in euphemisms of the period. Though the practice was not widely endorsed in public, demographics suggest that couples, even in rural areas, were taking initiatives in the nineteenth century to control the size of families.[18] This seems not to have been the case with Tillie and Con, however.

Despite her daily labors, Sarah had many pleasures in her life that she records in her diary. "The earth is full of lovlines. The air is perfumed with the sweet flowers. Oh so wonderfull is his mercy to the children of men. Words cannot express the addoration and grattitude I feel in sight of so much goodness and love," she wrote on June 14, 1870. She was moved by the beauties of the natural world around her and enjoyed cultivating flowers and swapping plants with her friends. A Lady Washington geranium, a southern rose, larkspur, oleander . . . all gave her great pleasure. She tended the flowers planted around the house, planted bulbs in the

---

[18] Brodie, pp. 4-6, 180-203. A comparison of the childbearing patterns of Sarah and her daughter Tillie, reveals that Sarah had her first child after 9 months of marriage and then had the other 4 children in intervals of 3, 4, 8, 5 years. Tillie had 8 children, the first born about 11 months after her marriage. Her subsequent children were born in intervals of 2 years and 3 months, 1 year and 10 months, 2 years and 1 month (twins), 2 years and 6 months, 7 years (this child died as a newborn), and 1 year and 2 months. It seems unlikely that Tillie and Con were attempting to space their children.

Tillie Reid Preston
(Daughter of Sarah Tabitha Reid, wife of Benjamin Conover Preston).
Monmouth County Historical Association Library and Archives

fall, and brought plants inside throughout the winter. In early December she still had blossoms enough to make a wedding bouquet of roses and pink verbenas for a friend. "They had it on the mantle piece in the parlor. It looked very nice," she noted contentedly in her diary at the end of the day on December 9, 1869.

Each entry of Sarah's diary begins with an account of the day's weather. Weather, of course, was a controlling feature of her day that deeply affected the conditions of her work and her ability to go about. Bad weather kept her from church and visiting, causing her to worry about the health and safety of the family and the farm animals. But her interest in the weather was aesthetic and spiritual as well. She reveled in the beauty of her natural surroundings and pondered the meaning of this beauty. "It rained until after dinner," she wrote on December 16, 1869, "and then it cleared off splendid. The afternoon was like a summers day and a splendid moonlight night likewise. What a beautiful earth our Heavenly Father has made for us to dwell in, and we so incensible to his goodness."

A feature of Sarah's diary that is common to many women's diaries is her record of the visitors who came to the farm and the visiting she and her family did in return. Personal visits were her primary form of communication with her relatives, friends, neighbors, and fellow members of the Old Tennent congregation. Letters were occasionally written and the telegraph used to reach William in New York City, but the principle medium of the family's relational network was personal visiting. Visits were for sharing work, to borrow or lend items, to give and receive information and news, to purchase, sell or exchange products and settle accounts, to comfort the sick and bereaved, to greet out-of-town visitors or a new baby, and in one case to put a stop to malicious gossip. If poor weather or poor health kept the family from visiting, they were cut off from their vital network of assistance and communication. Visits were rarely purely social occasions. In a life dominated by the demands of incessant work, only on the Sabbath or in the slack winter months, could Sarah undertake the luxury of a purely social call, and then infrequently. The patterns of the Reid family's visiting are typical of those revealed in other working people's diaries. In a study of antebellum working-class diaries in New England, sociologist Karen L. Hansen emphasizes the community importance of visiting:

> Visits recorded in diaries by both women and men involved the exchange of numerous goods and services. Purposeful and systematic but informal and unplanned, visits provided an occasion to cement ties and to exchange comfort, companionship, information, moral evaluations, entertainment, and labor. . . A focus on the more microsocial level of everyday face-face interaction is indispensable for understanding how the fabric of community life. . . was created and maintained by human action.[19]

Hansen's findings apply equally to the importance of visiting as revealed in Sarah's diary.

At the heart of the Reids' community life were Sarah's aunts, her mother's younger sisters, and their husbands: Harriet (Reid) and John Jewell who lived nearby, probably in Manalapan; Margaret (Reid) Van Cleve and her husband, Benjamin, who also lived nearby on the main road to Freehold; and Susan (Reid) and Gilbert Applegate who lived in Englishtown. A host of cousins of various ages formed a larger community of family associations. Neighbors, such as the Gravatts

---

[19] Karen L. Hansen, "Rediscovering the Social: Visiting Practices in Antebellum New England and the Limits of the Public/Private Dichotomy" in Jeff Weintraub and Krishan Kumar, *Public and Private in Thought and Practice* (Chicago: University of Chicago Press, 1997), p. 280.

and the Perrines, were a central part of the relationship circle, relied on for assistance and companionship and in turn relying on help from the Reids. "Had a call in the evening. Mr Apelgate called to borrow my mourning. He had lost a sister in law," Sarah wrote on May 18, 1869. And again, "Mrs Perine called and got some butter and engaged cream for the wedding to make ice cream," Sarah wrote on December 3, 1869. Trips to Freehold or Mount's Corner (West Freehold) were usually combined with visits to neighbors and relatives living along the way so that best use was made of the journey. Young people stopped by frequently, sometimes staying for meals, for overnight, or for several days to visit and help with work. Sarah's children in turn paid visits, stayed overnight and also presumably helped out.

Having a visitor did not require that work stop; quite the contrary. Often visitors came especially to work on a project. On May 6, 1869, Sarah wrote,

Went in the morning to uncle Benies and brought aunt Margaret & went to uncle Johny's and brout aunt Harriet home with me likewise and we cuilted a comfortable and finished it before four oclock. Had a very nice time. Enjoyed it very much.

When Mrs. Armes, a clergyman's widow, came to visit for a few days, she entered into the household work. Sarah wrote on September 7, 1869:

About half past nine in the morning Mr Combs brought Mrs Armes I was very glad to see her. She is such a good woman and one that has not a great deal of this worlds goods and so she was doubly welcome. She helped me with my peaches. Spent a very happy day.

Sometimes, however, visitors interrupted work in welcome ways. On June 17, 1870 she wrote,

The children done the breckfast dishes and I went in the seller to clean the floor. I paid Mrs Mack seventy five cents for doing it and the floor is worse than she commenced it. A complete mud lake. I had not scrubbed long when Mrs Samuel Conover & Fannie came. I was very glad to see them. They are peticular friends of mine, and so I discontinued my work in the celler. Spent the day very pleasantly with them. They took dinner & tea with me and went home a bout five oclock.

Visiting for Sarah was her social life. It took her away from the confines of her home and farm, and it also made her home a social space where others might appear at any time of the day or evening and expect to be sheltered and fed and to enter into the tasks at hand. Bad weather might cause someone to be "stormstaid" for the night, or the length of a journey might require a visit of several days. The quality of a person's interactions with callers and hosts determined to some extent the quality of one's reputation in the community, and visiting cemented important relationships. The hospitality of shelter and food was an important part of the visiting routine, offered regularly to any visitors, in addition to the family and hired hands. "Had a call. Mr Sam Davisson and his wife and cousin Miss Gravat. They took tea with me," Sarah wrote on June 20, 1869. Sending a visitor or worker away without food was a serious offense as Sarah indicated in her criticism of the wife of Elwood's employer on January 24, 1871:

> Clark Perines wife makes a bisness of rushing her breackfast table off of the floor on Sunday mornings to have two clerks that sleep in the store go without any breckfast. I do not thank her. She is a member of Mr Chandler church, but I think she has failed to make it her duty to pracktice the golden rule. My boy never had to go without his breakfast or supper in his life before and no child that I ever had black or white ever went to bed without supper or went without breckfast. I could not sleep if I had let any one go without their meals as she has repetedly.

As Sarah's life became more consumed with work both her reading and her visiting declined. "I stayed home from calling on my neighbors all summer to try to get my sewing done but I cannot without sewing in the time I should have to read," she recalled on January 14, 1871 as she was regretting the sacrifice of both her visiting and her reading to her work.

Sarah's religion was one of her greatest joys and comforts. Her daily routine was informed by her religious belief and observance. Her faith filled the empty spaces left by the absence of her older children and her husband, and was a source of solace when she was worried or exhausted by her life. She attended Sabbath services and sometimes Sabbath School as frequently as family demands and weather conditions would allow. She was an enthusiastic advocate of Rev. Archibald Cobb, the Old Tennent pastor at the time. Sunday sermons, religious reading, and hymn singing were favorite pastimes, as well as elements of her religious observance. Reading was particularly important to her. She occasionally read *Demorest's Illustrated Monthly and Mme. Demorest's Mirror of Fashions*, a popular family magazine that often included paper patterns for women's clothing, but the greater portion of her reading material was religious in nature. Her Bible was part of her private devotions as well as the family worship that was held in the evening. Sarah read books on religious subjects, usually classic devotional literature written by

---

[20] The books Sarah mentions specifically are Archibald Alexander, *Thoughts on Religious Experience*, first published in 1841; Philip Doddridge, *The Rise and Progress of Religion in the Soul*, first published in 1744; James Hamilton, *The Mount of Olives; and Other Lectures on Prayer*, 1846; and James Madison MacDonald's *My Father's House; or The Heaven of the Bible*, last published in 1869.

Presbyterian clergymen.[20] She also enjoyed the *Missionary Herald*, a monthly publication of the American Board of Foreign Missions that included reports of missions in exotic places, and the *New York Observer*, a well-established non-partisan Protestant newspaper published in New York City. Along with the news, it carried religious and sentimental poetry, some of which Sarah transcribed in her diary.

Hymn singing was a special joy and an emotional outlet for Sarah. She sang hymns with the children at home for recreation, as part of family evening devotions, and at church. She frequently quoted fragments of hymns in her diary, and recalled hymns that particularly moved her at church. On July 18, 1869 she wrote:

The second hymn that was sung was Jesus loveer of my soul a hymn I love so much I alway's shed tears when I sing it. It seems to express my feelings so much, and I love to sing it but I was so full I had to omit some lines. I could not sing for tears checked my utterances and I could not go on part of the time but I sung it through. The gentlemen all set facing me. I do not know what they thought I was crying about but my feelings are so tender and the second line made me almost burst in tears.

Singing was a pleasure for her children as well, and provided them with one of their few pleasurable entertainments. Elwood, the younger girls, and Sarah all went to local singing schools from time to time. Singing schools had became popular in the northeast after the Revolutionary War and continued to be a community resource well into the nineteenth century. Sometimes they were run by local people, sometimes by itinerant singing masters who would set up a school for a period of time and then move on when the market was saturated. Students learned to read music and basic vocal techniques using shape note notation in the early nineteenth century and later using modern musical notation. A lively hymn literature provided students with a repertoire that was particularly enjoyable to sing. Classes were also important social occasions and must have been a large part of the appeal of singing school for Elwood and the girls.[21]

Music was an important element in the worship at the Old Tennent Church. Traditionally congregational singing was led by "precenters" who lined out the verses of a hymn for the congregation to follow. As more people became conversant with sight reading of music, church choirs began to be formed. The Old Tennent Church had a church choir accompanied by instrumentalists to lead the singing as early as 1846. In 1856 an Estey & Green melodeon was installed in the church.

---

[21] Larry Gordon and Anthony G. Barrand, eds., *Northern Harmony* (Plainfield, VT: Northern Harmony Publishing Company, 1998), pp. ix-x. The Drew University Library holds a large collection of the song books used in nineteenth-century singing schools.

[22] Symmes, *Psalms and Hymns, Adapted to Social, Private, and Public Worship in the Presbyterian Church* (Philadelphia: Presbyterian Board of Publication, 1843), pp. 144-146.

Old Tennent Church, circa 1890s photograph by Stauffer, Asbury Park. Monmouth County Historical Association Library and Archives (T-25)

Sarah's minister, Archibald Cobb, was said to have had a fine singing voice and fostered singing during his pastorate. Most of the hymns Sarah quotes in her diary are found in the hymn book in use at the Old Tennent Church at the time.[22]

Sarah used her diary as a place for expressing her religious views and devotional reflections. She did not fear damnation. She had a positive, hopeful personal religion that led her to anticipate a restful and beautiful afterlife created by a personal God, the loving Father she had not had on earth. She strove for full devotion and obedience to Jesus; her favorite hymns were lively, with an almost sensual quality about them. What may have been, for her, an arid and lonely personal life, was relieved by a fully emotional religious life. Frequent in her journal entries are devotional passages of celebration or consolation written in words taken directly or paraphrased from the Bible and Presbyterian hymnology. For example, in May 16, 1869 she wrote:

> Some of the family was gone to sabbeth school and I was quite lonesome. I had a very sweet time reading about the saviour. Oh that I could love him more and see all my children serving him. If I had a thoughsand hearts they could never prais him enough. Oh speak half his prais or wondrous love. Oh for such love let rocks and hills their lasting silence break and all harmonious human tongs his lasting praises speak.

Sarah tried to live out her religious principles in her social relationships. She visited sick and dying people when she could. She proselytized the Jewish peddlers who stopped by her door. She extended charity to the needy.[23] Transients and vagrants, many of them immigrants, were given refuge on the farm from time to time. Over the course of the diary young boys, single German men, a lone German woman, and even a couple with a small child took refuge in the barn or house, were fed, and sometimes hired to work before moving on.[24] Hospitality was usually given to such "travellers" without reservation. When the lone German woman stole from the family, she was fed and allowed to wash up before she left, treated more like a guest than a thief. "Poor thing," Sarah commented, "if she had been trained right she would not have paid me in the way she did. She cried when she went away and was sorry I think."[25]

---

[23] Two destitute African-American families in the area were particular recipients of food and supplies from Sarah. She did not record their surnames that might have told us if these people were local folk or refugees from the Civil War. See entries for February 26, 1870 and April 2, 1871.

[24] The incidence of German-speaking transients, whom Sarah called "Duch," reflects the proximity of Monmouth County to the embarkation port of New York, and also the fact that Germans were second only to Irish among the foreign-born population of New Jersey at the time. See Rudolph J. Vecoli, *The People of New Jersey* (Princeton: D. Van Nostrand Co., 1965), pp. 280-281.

[25] See entry for March 7, 1871.

[26] All three of these diaries are Revolutionary War diaries – Carol F. Karlsen and Laurie Crumpacker, eds., *The Journal of Esther Edwards Burr*, 1754-1757 (1984): the mid-eighteenth century journal kept by Esther Edwards Burr, the daughter of Jonathan Edwards and wife of Aaron Burr, the second president of the College of New Jersey (now Princeton University); Margaret Hill Morris, *Private Journal, Kept During a Portion of the Revolutionary War* (1969): the Revolutionary war diary kept by Margaret Hill Morris, a Quaker who lived much of her life in Burlington and who commented extensively on the Battles of Trenton and Princeton; Jemima Condict Harrison, *Jemima Condict, Her Book*, 1772-1779 (1930): a diary kept when Jemima was a young unmarried woman recording her everyday concerns and the impact of the war on her daily life.

See also an unpublished war diary: Ann Cooper Whitall, *Typescript of her diary*, Frank H. Stewart Collection, Savitz Library, Rowan University. Ann Cooper Whitall's diary, which she began keeping

Private diaries like Sarah Reid's are not uncommon in local historical archives, but few of them reach public attention. Most diaries or journals by New Jersey women that have reached public attention, such as those of Esther Edwards Burr, Jemima Condict, or Margaret Hill Morris, do so because their writers were part of a well-educated elite, were close to the central actors in the historical events of their day, or self-consciously recorded observations of historical events.[26] These diaries often stand on their own, and their historical content is easily accessible. Rarely do the diaries of women like Sarah Reid, chronicling the lives of everyday people, of working people, or people otherwise invisible in the historical record, see the light of day. Yet such diaries give us a wealth of historical information about the realities of daily work and life, the thought and spiritual concerns of less educated people, and the interconnections between individuals and families in local communities. The diaries of everyday women literally give voice to women from the past; we hear their language and feel the heat of their intimate expression. Such diaries were not written with the thought that they might have an audience or be part of the historical record. As a result, few have been preserved and published, to the detriment of our historical understanding. We are fortunate to be privy to Sarah Reid's world.[27]

EPILOGUE

After the close of Sarah Reid's diary our only information about her family comes from the public record. The major depression that plagued the country between 1873 and 1878 took a toll on the nation's farmers that Sarah and William must have felt deeply. Apparently Tillie and Con never did take over the farming of the family farm, for Sarah and William sold their farmland, heavily mortgaged, in 1878. It is unclear exactly where they made their home after leaving the farm in

---

in 1760 as a daily record and spiritual journal, became a valuable historical source on Revolutionary conflict in Gloucester County area because, as a Quaker pacifist, she chose to stay in her home and record events. [All four women are profiled in Joan N. Burstyn, *Past and Promise: Lives of New Jersey Women* (Syracuse: Syracuse University Press, 1997).]

[27] Two important unpublished New Jersey women's diaries of this sort, written earlier in the nineteenth century, are those of Elizabeth Mulford Crane of Berkeley Heights (Elizabeth Mulford Crane, Diary Typescript, Special Collections/University Archives, Alexander Library, Rutgers University) and Sarah Staats Bayles of South Bound Brook (Sarah Staats Bayles, Daybook, Special Collections/ University Archives, Alexander Library, Rutgers University). Elizabeth Crane, the wife of a local farmer, began her diary in 1824 when she was 49. She used it to record the weather and her work weaving and making clothes, carpets, and binding shoes. Crane and her husband converted to Methodism in 1806 and her diary records her experience at early camp meetings in the 1820s. Sarah Bayles also kept her diary in her middle age from 1839-1850. Like Sarah Reid, she was a Presbyterian. Bayles' diary is of particular interest because she left her alcoholic husband early in her marriage and returned to her family farm with her one child. She spent the rest of her life helping her father and brother maintain the farm. Her fragmentary diary records the daily events on the farm and in her church. Both these diaries are of particular local interest, and though written earlier in the century than Sarah Reid's, reveal the daily texture of farm life. [Both women are profiled in Joan N. Burstyn, *Past and Promise: Lives of New Jersey Women* (Syracuse: Syracuse University Press, 1997).]

1879, though they are listed in the 1880 United States Census of Manalapan. Despite Sarah's fretting about the condition of her children's souls, they all eventually joined the Old Tennent Church; Tillie and Con in 1872, Florence and Lizzie in 1876 and Elwood in 1877.[28] Tillie and Con had three more children: a daughter born in August 1873, another daughter born in 1880 who died as an infant, and a son born in 1881. Elwood was still living at home early in 1880, but was married in Red Bank in November of that year to Mary F. McLean. They lived in Englishtown where he was in business for 40 years and also postmaster for 16 years; they had four children. Lizzie was also still living at home in 1880 though she married at the rather advanced age of 24 in May of the next year to Charles F. McDonald. They lived in Englishtown where Charles became County Collector. They had three children. No doubt, it would have been comforting for Sarah to know that her struggles with Lizzie were not ultimately in vain; when Lizzie died in 1916, she was remembered as "a highly educated woman and a great reader. She was especially loved at Englishtown for her works of charity. She had long been a member of Englishtown Presbyterian Church and was active in various societies and prominent in all phases of church work."[29] Little Florence married in February 1881, just three days after her 17th birthday to William M. Rankin; they eventually lived in Manasquan and had five children.

Sarah Reid died of double pneumonia four months after her 68th birthday on March 16, 1888 in Wall Township, her last place of residence. She was the grandmother of 20 children, 15 of whom were born before she died. William Reid lived to the age of 77 and died at his daughter Florence's home in Manasquan on August 29, 1894. Sarah and William are buried in the Old Tennent Church Yard, as are Elwood, Lizzie and Tillie.

Each of Sarah's daughters named a daughter for her, but it was Florence, the youngest, who preserved her mother's diary. It passed to her daughter Sarah E. (Rankin) Axelby, who lived in Indianapolis, and then to Sarah Axelby's only child, William Axelby. When William died in April 1992 without an heir, his great grandmother's diary went to friends who recognized its historical value and returned it to Monmouth County.

[28] Symmes, pp. 198, 200.
[29] *Freehold Transcript*, July 28, 1916, p. 3.

EDITING THE MANUSCRIPT

Sarah Reid kept her diary in a lined, leather-bound ledger. The 9 x 13 3/4 x 1/2 inch ledger had been used for other record keeping before she started her diary, so she cut away the used portions of the pages and wrote her entries frugally in the remaining space. The diary begins with a title page:

Mrs. Sarah Tabitha Reid

April 19, 1869

West Freehold

Diary

Embedded in the September 1869 entries, are several entries dated November 1868, suggesting that at an earlier time Sarah was randomly keeping a diary. I have placed these 1868 entries at the beginning of the transcribed diary, to preserve the chronology of events. Sarah's diary was unpaginated and ordered simply by the chronology of the entries. Some entries were misdated. Where this was the case, I have assumed that day of the week is the more likely indicator and have corrected the dates accordingly, adding the actual date in brackets.

Sarah kept her diary quite faithfully during 1869 and 1870. In 1871 she wrote entries into early May, made two entries in July, and then picked up her writing again in late November, leaving out entries for the busiest time of the farming calendar. The body of the diary ends on December 27, 1871. There is one entry for January 23, 1872, and then two more entries, one dated simply 1873, and one dated December 26 with no year.

In an effort to preserve the authenticity of the diary I have made as few editorial alterations as possible, making changes only when necessary to enhance its readability. Sarah did not write in defined sentences and she sometimes used a comma instead of a period to end a thought. I have imposed sentence breaks where a thought clearly indicates, adding capitalization and periods to achieve this. Occasionally Sarah used paragraph indentations to separate thoughts–these have been retained. Sarah's spelling, capitalization, and other forms of punctuation have been retained. Sarah frequently left "t" uncrossed and used a printed two-hump m instead of the cursive three-hump "m." These irregularities have been standardized as have been occasional slips of the pen, such as duplicated words and extraneous letters. Words she crossed out have been omitted. Her infrequent marginal notes are included in italics within the appropriate entry.

Brackets have been used editorially in several ways. When Sarah omitted a word, the omission is indicated by [. . .]; when a word is undecipherable it is indicated by [?]; when a word was left incomplete it is completed, as in El[wood]; when dates were incorrect, the correct date is supplied within brackets [September 9]; and finally, when Sarah's spelling might be entirely baffling, the modern spelling of the word is supplied in brackets.

I have attempted to clarify the text by supplying footnotes identifying people and places where possible; by supplying the meaning of unfamiliar or archaic words; and by adding historical information where it seems appropriate and useful.[30]

[30] For biographical identification I have relied primarily on the following sources: Beers Atlas of 1873; Franklin Ellis, History of Monmouth County (Philadelphia: 1885. Reprint facsimile, 1974); Medical Society of New Jersey, Transactions; Presbyterian Synod of New Jersey, Minutes for the Year ending 1869, Minutes for year 1870 (New Brunswick: 1869, 1870); Princeton Theological Seminary, Biographical Catalogue (Princeton: Theological Seminary of the Presbyterian Church, 1933); Frank R. Symmes, History of Old Tennent Church (Cranbury: George W. Burroughs, 1904); Eileen Jourdan Thompson, "Some Ancestors and Descendants of Sarah Tabitha Reid of West Freehold, New Jersey", Monmouth Country Historical Association; United States, Manuscript Census, Monmouth County, New Jersey, 1870; Western Theological Seminary, Historical and Biographical Catalogue (Allegheny, PA: The Seminary, 1885).

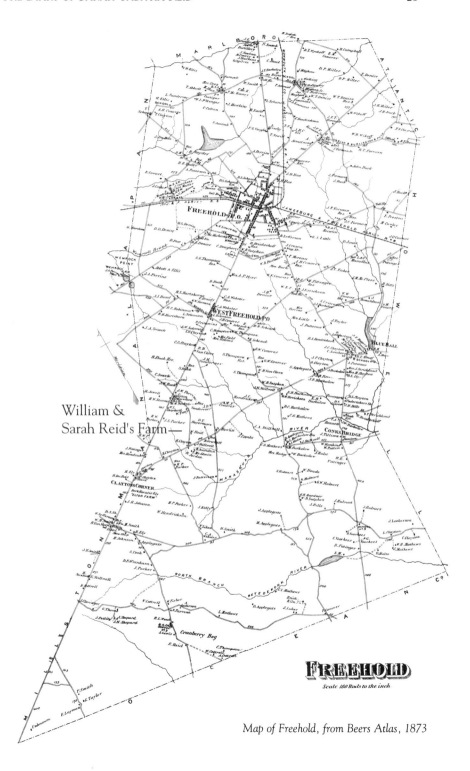

William &
Sarah Reid's Farm —

Map of Freehold, from Beers Atlas, 1873

THE DIARY

Nov 20 friday 1868

Pleasant day. All well. Mended the most of the day. Wanted to go to uncle johnys[1] but could not go.

Nov 21 Saturday

Cool and blustery. Wanted so much to go to Mr Storms[2] funeral but Elwood[3] had made an engagement to go a gunning and so I was disapointed. He was a near neighbor and died very suddon. How little do we know when [. . .] may be at the door. We ought to be so kind to our dear ones while we have them and bear so patient with their infirmaties. We are all of us faulty and ought to see our own faults so much plainer than we do those of others so we may have a chance to correct them. In the evening Joe Clayton & Sally Hendricksson called on horse back. Elwood took a ride with them. I received a letter from Mr William H[4] in the evening and was so glad to hear from him and hear he is soon to be home.

Nov 22 Sabbeth

A cool day. Went to the old tennet church and herd mr Cob[5] preach a very good sermon on being charitable. He need not preached it to me. I am grieved anough that I have so little to give. I have saved the sugar out of my tea and coffee ever since I was maried so I would have something for the mishionaries and yet I have done so little for them and they suffering so much for the dear saviours cause. I would like so much to have something to give to them and aged ministers that has spent their lives in my masters service. Mr Vlet rode home from church with us.

Nov 23 Monday

A very beautiful day. Went about ten oclock over to uncle Johny's to help them fix for prayer meeting. Walked there and back again and helped them what

---

[1] John Reid Jewell (1802-1890): Sarah's uncle by marriage. He was married to Harriet (Reid) (1802-1883), Sarah's maternal aunt.

[2] A neighbor who lived on the main road to Freehold.

[3] William Elwood Tennent Reid (1848-1930): Sarah's only son. He was twenty at the time.

[4] Sarah's husband, William H. Reid (1817-1894), worked in New York City, presumably as a bricklayer. He traveled into the city by train and was gone the better part of the year, April through December. Sarah consistently referred to him as "Mr. Reid."

[5] The Reids attended the Old Tennent Church, an historic Presbyterian church on the road from Freehold to Englishtown. The minister of the church was the Rev. Archibald Parritt Cobb (1821-1881) who was the pastor from 1863-1881. He graduated from Princeton College in 1850 and studied for two years at the Princeton Theological Seminary. He was licensed to preach in 1853.

I could. Dressed and went to prayer meeting. Had a very good one as Mr Cob always has. Baptised three of Charlies Jewels[6] little children.

Nov 24 Tuesday

A very splendid sunrise. A warm beautiful day. Finished my dress almost in the morning & went in the afternoon to call on Mrs William H Parkers[7] has a beautiful little girl of two weeks old. Called likewise on Mrs Shepherd.[8] Was very much pleased with her. Went in the evening to see fannie Conover.[9] She is very sick with the tiphoid fever. Had a pressent of some nice cranberies from her mother.

Nov 25 Wensday

A very eleghant day. Sewed some in the morning. Made some pies and swept the yard in the afternoon. All well and tomorrow is thanksgiving & Mr Reid is coming. I shall be very glad to see him safe home once more.

[6] Charles Symmes Jewell: a commission merchant in Manalapan. He was a son of John and Harriet Jewell and Sarah's first cousin.

[7] Mary Elizabeth (Reid) Parker: a cousin of Sarah and William's and a neighbor on the main road to Freehold.

[8] A neighbor on the main road to Freehold.

[9] Fannie Conover: Sarah's niece, the daughter of Matilda (Reid) and Samuel Conover, Sarah's sister-in-law.

Mrs. Sarah Tabitha Reid

West freehold

Diary

Aprail 29 1869 [Thursday]

A very chill cloudy day. Rained some. I expected to clean a bed room but it
was too stormy. I spent the day quilting with my little girls.[10] Was disapointed
about going to prayer meeting as it was the last night it was to be held. I am very
sorry it is a going to break up. It was such a comfort to know there was worship
in the school house, and I liked so much to join them in praising his precious
name.

Aprail 30 friday

A pleasant day. About eleven oclock we saw Mr Reid coming home. We was
so glad to see him safe home. I spent the morning in sweeping the chamber. In
the afternoon Mr Reid took me and the children to Freehold, and he bought
him a new hat and I bought me a lady washington gerraneum.

May 1 Saturday

A very stormy day. I was baking and busy all day. All well and very happy Mr
Reid was home.

May 2 Sabbeth

A stormy morning and so far to go to church we could not go. We spent a
very happy day alone with our little ones. The children learned some catechism.
I spent some of the time reading Elixandders religious Experience.[11]

---

[10] Sarah had two young daughters living at home at the time: Margaret Elizabeth Reid (1857-1916)
known as Lizzie, who was going on twelve, and Florence Augusta Reid (1862-1934) often called Flora
and then later Gussie or Augusta, who was seven.

[11] Archibald Alexander, D.D., *Thoughts on Religious Experience*, was a highly regarded devotional guide
first published in 1841. Alexander (1772-1851), a Presbyterian clergyman, educator and author, was
the first professor of the Princeton Theological Seminary, elected in 1812.

May 3 Monday

A cold blusterry day. Arose before five in the morning. Mr Reid went to new york,[12] I could not persuade him to stay at home. He said it was his duty to go, but my trust is in God he is able to keep him safe any where.

I spent part of the night in prayer, I was so anxious that God should keep him from all harm and prepare him for his heavenly kingdom.

I shed many tears over him and my only son who will not give the morning of his days to the dear saviour. It grieves me so much to have infinite love slited and rejected so long by those whose first words was to lisp the saviour prais. I have always antisapated that my children would love the saviour early. I have espected they would serve the saviour from their childhood. They have shid so many tears over the saviours love and suffering.

May 4 Tuesday

Nice day. Washed. All well.

May 5 Wednesday

Very beautiful day. Worked in the garden. Hoed some and planted flower seeds. Went in the evening about five oclock to uncle Johny Jewell, had a very pleasant call.

May 6 thursday

Went in the morning to uncle Benies and brought aunt Margaret[13] & went to uncle Johny's and brout aunt Harriet home with me likewise and we cuilted a comfortable[14] and finished it before four oclock. Had a very nice time. Enjoyed it very much.

May 7 friday

Very warm beautiful day. Cleaned two rooms in the chamber. I whitewashed them. Very tired at night.

---

[12] William Reid's commute to and from New York was done by railroad. He would have taken the Freehold & Jamesburg Agricultural Railroad to Jamesburg where it connected to the Camden and Amboy. Riders could go either north to New York or south to Trenton and Philadelphia. The Freehold and Jamesburg was the first railroad in Monmouth County when it began operation in 1853, in response to the growth of the commercial marl industry and increased demands for getting agricultural products to market.

[13] Benjamin B. and Margaret (Reid) Van Cleve were Sarah's uncle by marriage and maternal aunt. They lived not far from Sarah on the main road to Freehold.

[14] A comforter.

May 8 Saturday

Very nice day. Baked in the morning. Very busy all day. Received a letter from W H Reid.[15]

May 9 Sabbeth

Very beautiful day. Went to church. Heard a young minister preach. The children went to sabbeth school in the afternoon.

May 10 Monday

Elmira[16] came back about nine oclock in the morning. We washed in the morning. In the afternoon we went to Garret Denices[17] and bought Elmira a hat. Had a nice ride. Lost one of my little goslings when I came back. I was very sorry about it.

May 11 Tuesday

Cleaned my bed room. Beautiful day. Elmira cleaned the floor. I done the white washing.[18]

May 12 Wednesday

Whitewashed Elmira bed room and hall. I was very tired.

May 13 Thursday

Cleaned and straightened the clothes room and mended some. A very splendid shower in the afternoon. Elwood went in the carriage for the children to school[19] and brought them home. Elmira finished her ironing.

May 14 Friday

A very bright beautiful morning. I baked in the morning. Made bread pies two kinds of cake and rice pudding. Cleaned the pantry and mended Elwoods coat. Went out and was caught in a shower. We had a splendid shower. Monroe Hendricks called. Very busy day, but God is so good. Oh what mercy flows from heaven.

---

[15] W. H. Reid: Sarah's husband, William H. Reid.

[16] Elmira was employed to help with the heavier housework, such as washing, ironing, and floor washing. It was not uncommon for young farm women to hire out as household help and Elmira may have been Elmira Gravatt, the 19-year-old daughter of close neighbors, Benjamin and Sarah Gravatt.

[17] Garret Denise: a merchant with a store in Manalapan village.

[18] Sarah regularly whitewashed the rooms of her house. Whitewash was a substitute for paint made at home by pouring boiling water over lime and adding sulphate of zinc and salt to cause the wash to harden without cracking. Colorings could be added to tint the white wash.

[19] Florence and Lizzie probably went to the schoolhouse at West Freehold [Mount's Corners].

May 15 Saturday

A splendid cool morning. I was up pretty early. Went out after breakfast and set some hens.[20] Came in and commenced cleaning the parlor. Miss Lizzie Perine[21] called quite early. I was very glad to see her. After dinner Elwood went to make Tillie[22] a visit. We do not expect him home until tomorrow. Lillie went away after dinner also. Mrs Appelgate[23] called this afternoon. I was not done cleaning. I was very sorry. I finished about three oclock. Read some in that Demorests book[24] after I comed my head. Fed my little chickens and worked in the garden after tea. Planted summer saviory [savory] and beet seed each and set out some onions Mrs Perine[25] sent me this afternoon with Lizzie Reid. I have not herd from Mr Reid since last Saturday evening. I do want to hear very much. I expect there is a letter at the store at west freehold but I have no one to go for it.

May 16 Sabbeth

Showery in the afternoon. Had a hail storm and a gust of wind with it. After that a splendid shower and the most splendid bow of promise[26] was ever seen. It spaned the heavens and was so very brilliant and a small one near.

I was all alone. Some of the family was gone to sabbeth school and I was quite lonesome. I had a very sweet time reading about the saviour. Oh that I could love him more and see all my children serving him. If I had a thoughsand hearts they could never prais him enough. Oh speak half his prais or wondrous love. Oh for such love let rocks and hills their lasting silence break and all harmonious human tongs his lasting praises speak.

May 17 Monday

A windy cool day. Very busy washing and cleaning the sitting room. The children helped me with the windows and floor.

---

[20] Hens were "set" on nests with eggs to brood and hatch the chicks.

[21] Lizzie Perrine: the eldest daughter of James W. and Deborah Perrine, neighbors who lived at the corner of Sarah's road and the main road to Freehold. Perrine was a common name in the area, and various Perrines figure throughout Sarah's diary.

[22] Tillie: Sarah's eldest child, Matilda Reid Preston (1845-1930), who was married to Benjamin Conover Preston, usually called Con. Tillie and Con lived some distance away, probably in the vicinity of Englishtown, and had four small children.

[23] Many Applegates figure in Sarah's diary. Some were probably relatives of Sarah's uncle, Gilbert Applegate.

[24] *Demorest's Illustrated Monthly* and *Mme. Demorest's Mirror of Fashions* was a popular family magazine in the later nineteenth century. It often included paper patterns for women's clothing.

[25] Mrs. Perrine: probably Deborah Perrine, a neighbor.

[26] Bow of promise: rainbow.

May 18 Tuesday

A dull cool day. Straightened up the sitting [room] and commenced Ellie a shirt. In the afternoon Lizzie Perine called, and Ellie [Elwood] took Hannah Gravat[27] to Garret Denices and came back before six in the evening. Had a call in the evening. Mr Apelgate called to borrow my mourning.[28] He had lost a sister in law.

May 19 Wednesday

A cold stormy day. I finished Elwoods shirt and done some other sewing. Read some in Madam Demorest [*Demorest's Illustrated Monthly*] book and baked in the morning.

May 20 Thursday

A nice day. Sewed some. Watched my turkeys and seen to my chickens. Basted and sewed bosom[29] for Mr Reid.

May 21 friday 1868

A dull day. Elmira went home in the morning with the head ache and I done the work and fixed to bake and sewed some in the afternoon. Washed some in the morning. Received a letter from Mr Reid last evening.

Saturday 22 May

Very busy in the morning. My two dear little girls helped me bake iron some and churn. Elmira went away before the ironing was done and came back in the afternoon and cleaned the citchen. I went in the afternoon to freehold with Elwood and Lizzie Perine. Had a splendid ride. Went to the flower garden of Mr Monroes[30] in the evening. Idy Reid[31] came with his cousin to see Elwood and went away sabbeth evening.

May 23 Sabbeth

A very eleghant morning but I could not go to church because I had no one to drive for me. Had not much time to read on Gods holy day.

---

[27] Hannah Gravat: the 17-year-old daughter of the neighboring Gravatt family.

[28] Mourning and funeral practices were highly ritualized in the nineteenth century, and articles of mourning attire would have been borrowed back and forth as circumstances required.

[29] Shirt front.

[30] Sarah is probably referring to the gardens and greenhouse of P. J. Moreau, a commercial nurseryman in Freehold.

[31] Idy Reid: Many young Reids who have not been identified visited the Reids throughout the time of the diary. Some may have been Sarah's relatives, some William's.

May 24 Monday

A beautiful day. Washed in the morning. I read some in the afternoon. Rote a letter in the evening to my husband.

May 25 Tuesday

A very splendid day. Churned in the morning. Lizzie Perine spent the afternoon with me and made Lizzie a white lace hat. Had a nice time with her. She made the hat splendid. A beautiful moonlight night.

May 26 wensday

A nice day. Very warm. I was very busy making a white vest for Elwood, & Elmira was ironing and fixing[12] to go to her cousins wedding. Towards sundown the sky grew very dark and we had a very great blow and afterwards a very sweet shower.

May 27 Thursday

A very dul morning. Started about nine in the morning to go to see Mrs Spafford Reids.[13] Arived there after eleven oclock. Had a very nice visit. She stitched two shirt bosoms very beautiful for me. She has the sweetest babe ever was seen. It is five months old and so good natured and pleasant. It draws its sweet mouth every time you look at it.

May 28 friday

A dull raining morning. Very busy baking and set some hens in the morning. Baked bread two kinds of cake four pies and a puding in the afternoon. I almost made a fine shirt for Mr Reid. There was a little done to it and the bosom was ready. I worked hard all day. I don't mind work. It is a pleasure to me to be able to work and it is one of Gods greatest blessing's. We ought to be very happy when surrounded with so many blessings. Mr James Perine[14] called in the evening. It is still raining a fine drisly rain at eight oclock. Goodness and mercy has always surrounded my path

How manifold are thy works, what a merciful God we have. What would I do if I had no helper to go to. How would a poor blind mortle direct his steps aright in this world of snares and temptations with no omnipotent arm to lead us on from earth to heaven.

[12] Fixing: a colloquialism meaning to get ready, to prepare.
[13] Mrs. Spafford Reid: Hannah (Miller) Reid, Sarah's sister-in-law, the wife of William Reid's younger brother G. Spafford Reid.
[14] James A. Perrine: a neighbor, and father of Lizzie Perrine.

Saturday 29 May

A nice clear Morning. I white washed the kitchen and helped Elmira clean the windows. Made all straight before Mr Reid came in the five oclock train. I was so happy to have him come home safe. I rejoice so much that I have such a kind father that will watch over my dear ones when they are squandered away from me.

May 30 Sabbeth

A very chill morning. I was part dressed for church when it looked dark and commenced to rain but did not rain much. Tillie and her husband and four little ones came about eleven oclock.[35] I had a nice time with them. Tillie has so much to do she is wore down so much I am affraid she will not see the summer out. I would willingly take one of her children and keep it for her if she could spare it.

May 31 Monday

A very eleghan day. We washed in the Morning, and in the afternoon I sewed on the childrens dresses and we had a very pleasant call from Acksia Perine.[36] Elwood went to Tillies and did not get home until eleven oclock. We had a gust about dusk and it rained hard all the evening. He had to put up under a shed until it slacked up. Mr Reid went to new york in the morning. I was sorry to have him go away. We need him home so much. It is so hard for him to go from home to make a living and my children is not alway's very polite to me. They think it a great trouble to help me in little things and it is such a pleasure to me to be able to work for them and wait on them as long as I am able. Unkind words wounds me to the very heart. I have always tried so hard to pleas my family it has been my greatest pleasure next to serving God to make my family happy in every way I could, and bear all my little cares pleasantly.

June 1 Tuesday

A nice day. Elmira and me went in the afternoon to freehold and bought her a dress.[37] Had a splendid ride. Arived home about seven ocloc.

June 2 Wednesday

A nice morning. Cut elmira dress in the morning. Sewed on lizzies dress in the afternoon.

---

[35] Sarah's daughter Tillie was 24 years old at the time. Her children were Sarah Frances (Fanny), aged 4 1/2, Cora Elizabeth, aged 2, and twins, Joseph Henry and William Elwood, aged 5 months old.

[36] Another member of the Perrine family.

[37] Sarah is referring to buying fabric to make a dress.

June 3 Thursday

A splendid morning. Went to Tillies with my little girls. Had a splendid ride. Drove myself. Drove patchie and jennie.[18] Called at Garrets store. Had a beautiful time. Did not get home until after dark.

June 4 friday

Baked in the morning. In the afternoon Kate Perine[19] called and spent the afternoon and made Lizzie a white lace hat. Very nice beautiful.

June 5 Saturday

Very busy ironing and baking pies and cake in the stove. In the afternoon I finished Lizzies dress. Had a hard shower in the afternoon. Two Mr Shepherds was here hoing potatoes.[40]

June 6 Sabbeth

A beautiful morning. Went with Elwood and my two little girls to church. Herd the sermon to children from Mr Cob. Very good.

June 7 Monday

A splendid day. We picked strawberries for market.[41] Three crates.

June 8 Tuesday

Very nice day. I baked in the oven. Aunt Margaret and uncle called to see me. Did not stay long.

June 9 wednesday

A very cold day. We picked strawberies in the morning. In the afternoon I mended some clothes. Swept the yard in the evening. Have twenty one little turkeys and about one hundred little chickens. We sent two crates.

June 10 thursday

Nice day. Elmira Ironed. We had the two Mr Shepherds here. I mended clothes.

---

[18] Patchie and Jennie were Sarah's favorite horses.

[39] Another member of the Perrine family.

[40] Thompson and James Shepherd: laborers who lived in the neighboring Shepherd household on the main road to Freehold. They worked as hired hands on the farm from time to time.

[41] The presence of the Jamesburg & Freehold Agricultural Railroad through Freehold made farming for the New York market an attractive business for area farmers.

June 11 friday

A beautiful day. Was very busy baking and fixing for Tillie and Mrs Duncan.

June 12 Saturday

Very beautiful day. Was disapointed my company did not come to dinner. Tillie and her family came to tea and expect to stay three or four days. Elmira went to Martha.[42]

June 13 Sabbeth

Conover[43] went away about ten oclock. He was not very well Tillie and her four little children was here. We had a splendid time. Johny Reid was here all night and him and Charly Gravet to dinner and Mary Reids Johny call in the afternoon.[44]

June 14 Monday

A very rainy day. In the afternoon it cleared off and Mr Reid came home in the afternoon train. I was so glad to see him. I had been thinking all day he would come home.

June 15 Tuesday

A nice day. Took a ride with Mr Reid in the afternoon. Washed some in the morning.

June 16 Wednesday

A splendid day. Arose very early. Mr Reid went to Newyork in the morning train. We picked one crate of strawberies and I took Tillie home in the afternoon.

June 17 Thursday

Came home from Conovers in the morning and fetched Fannie[45] with me. A very warm day. The children had broke my splendid sizsors that Mr Reid made me a present of. I was so much grieved about them. I thought they was so good and cost so much they would last me my life time and I was so careful of them.

---

[42] Martha: probably Martha Jemison Jewell, the daughter-in-law of Sarah's Uncle Johnny and Aunt Harriet. Martha was married to William Henry Jewell, a butcher, and had two young daughters, Hattie and Lizzie.

[43] Benjamin Conover Preston was Sarah's son-in-law.

[44] Charlie Gravatt: a member of the neighboring Gravatt family; the two John Reids were young cousins.

[45] Fannie: Sarah's 4 year-old granddaughter.

June 18 friday

Very busy day. Picked one crate of strawberries. Churned in the afternoon and ironed. Got tea and fixed for baking. A very eleghant night. The earth and sky is superbly splendid. I turned the lamp down so I could enjoy the beautiful earth My Heavenly Father has made so splendid for poor mortal man so unworthy his love and care. A very warm night but very light.

June 19 Saturday

A very warm sultry morning and very warm day and I do not think I never had such a hard time to get a big days work done. No help but my two little girls one eleven and the other one nine[46] and just as hllthy and fleshy as they can be but they do not like to work on a warm day and so I had a dredful time to get any thing done by them. I baked bread and custard pies and two kinds of cake and dinner to get and churning and the citchen to clean and straw berry jelly to make besides a great many things two numerous to mention and now it is twenty minutes of eleven and I have finished a black lace hat for my self and have yet to read my chapter and say my prayers which I have followed up since I was a little girl without Father or Mother in my Granmas house and one little brother.

> The Lord is my shepherd
> I shall not want, he always has
> kept me and always will.
>> blessed be his holy name
>> and let all the earth be filled
>> with his glory.

June 20 Sabbeth 1869

A very warm beautiful day. Went with Elwood and little Fannie to church. Herd a very splendid serm[on] from a stranger. Came home. Had a call. Mr Sam Davisson and his wife and cousin Miss Gravat. They took tea with me.

June 21 Monday

A nice day. Lizzie went to school and I had a busy day and no help.[47] Called on aunt harriet in the evening. Rain in the afternoon.

---

[46] Inexplicably Sarah was mistaken about Florence's age. Florence was born on February 20, 1862 making her 7 years, 4 months at the time.

[47] Lizzie and Flora went to school sporadically. Since compulsory school attendance was not mandated by the New Jersey legislature until 1875, children went to school when they chose or when their parents could spare them.

June 22 Tuesday

Baked in the morning and went to freehold in the afternoon. Had company to tea John Anderson and Calvin Reid. Received a letter from Mr Reid.

June 23 Wednesday

A very warm day. Lizzie went to school in the morning and came home at noon very wet coming through Mr Parkers grass and Elwood and her had a falling out about her shoe and I could not persuade her to go to the examination of the school and so we was all disapointed and I felt very badly about it.

June 24 Thursday

We was very busy washing. My two little girls helped me. It was a nice day. We worked very hard. Very warm day.

June 25 friday

A very warm day. I baked and churned and a great many other things.

June 26 Saturday

A very warm day. Lizzie cleaned the citchen floor and Flora cleaned the breckfast table and I ironed and the children and gerogis Lites[48] helped churn.

June 27 Sabbeth

Elwood & the children started for church but thought he was two late and went to his aunt mary Reids[49] & me and little Fannie was all alone all sabbeth night until nine oclock monday morning. I was very loneson but I new the same kind eyes was watching over me that has alway's a quieted me through all my days and in infancy. Elmira came in the morning about eight oclock. We canned gooseberries thirteen cans and cooked for men in the hay field. A very beautiful day. Is the 28 of June.

June 29 Tuesday

A very nice day. We washed a very a good large washing.

June 30 wednesday

A showery day. We did not get the cloths dry. The horses was in the corn and weet. Sallie Gravat[50] was here in the afternoon.

---

[48] Probably George Likes: the 11-year-old son of Timothy Likes, a distant neighbor.

[49] Mary Ely Reid: William Reid's sister-in-law.

[50] Sallie Gravat: the 15-year-old daughter in the neighboring Gravatt family.

July 1 [Thursday]

A nice day. I sewed some on a new calico dress. Cooked cherries. All well.

July 2 friday

A nice day. I was not very well in the morning. Elmira lost one day. Came in the afternoon and commenced ironing.

July 3 Saturday

A very fine day. We was very busy baking pies pudding and cake. Elmira ironed some in the morning. In the afternoon Mr Reid came home. We was so glad to see him safe home.

July fourth Sabbeth

A splendid morning. Cool and eleghant. Mr Reid wanted to see his daughter Tillie so much he went to see her. Had a beautiful ride. They was all well. I did not want to go but Mr. Reid would not hear of my staying home and I was so wore out for rest. I had worked so hard all the week.

July fifth Monday

A very beautiful cool day. Mr Reid and Elly cut his weet and we washed and I fixed to bake. Very busy all day, and one of my beautiful geese is dead. I am so sorry I did not think so much of them.

July 6 Tuesday

A very splendid cool day. I arose early and ironed some shirts for Mr Reid and then baked bread and fixed Mr Reids coat. Very busy all day. Went to freehold in the afternoon with Mr Reid. Took a pot of butter[51] and bought Lizzie and Florra a dress. Had a splendid ride.

July 7 Wednesday

Nice day. Sewed on my dress. Elmira ironed.

July 8 Thursday

A nice day. Charly Gravat helped Elwood and I finished my dress and fix to bake.

July 9 friday

A dull rainy day. Baked in the morning. Charly Gravat & Fred Bearmores[52] helped Elwood.

---

[51] Selling or trading butter was an important source of income for farm wives.

[52] The Bearmores, like the Gravatts, were close neighbors; Fred was their 15-year-old son.

July 10 Saturday

A beautiful cool day. Churned in the morning. Caned cherries in the afternoon six cans and done housework and cooked. Called to see aunt Harriet.

July 11 Sabbeth

A very eleghant day. Did not go to church, I wanted to go but Jennie was not shod and El[wood] thought she could not travel. I enjoyed Gods sweet day of rest. It was a nice rest to me. Help me my Father to love and serve thee. Thou art so good and merciful, the sweet words came in my head in the afternoon.

> Jesus the visions
> Jesus the visions of thy face
> Hath over powering charms
> Scarsce should I feel deaths cold embrace
> If Christ be in my arms.[53]

July 12 Monday

A beautiful day. I churned and cooked and done housework. Cad & El Gravat[54] was here carting in weet Made ice cream in the afternoon.

July 13 Tuesday

A splendid day. Went to freehold and bought me a dress in the morning. In the afternoon called on Mrs Perine. A letter from my husband.

July 14 wednesday

A dull rainy day. Churned and got breakfast and was ready to go to sewing a quarter before eight oclock. Sewed on my dress. Aunt Margaret called.

July 15 Thursday

Sewed on my dress and sent for elmira to come on friday morning.

July 16 friday

Elmira came in the morning and washed some and ironed some. Acksia Perine spent the afternoon with us and sewed on my dress.

---

[53] Sarah is recalling the fourth verse of a hymn by Isaac Watts, "Lord, at Thy temple we appear," first published in 1707. It appeared as hymn #618 in *Psalms and Hymns, Adapted to Social, Private, and Public Worship in the Presbyterian Church* (Philadelphia: Presbyterian Board of Publication, 1843). This was the hymnal in use at the Old Tennent Church at the time. Sarah quotes the verse again on April 5, 1870 with slightly different wording. The actual wording is "Jesus! The vision of Thy face, / Hath over-powering charms!/ Scarce shall I feel death's cold embrace, / If Christ be in my arms."

[54] Cad & El Gravat: Cad might have been a nickname for 25-year-old Charles Gravatt. El might have been his 19 year-old sister Elmira, come to help with the wheat harvest.

July 17 Saturday

A nice day. Very busy. Baked & ironed in the morning and sewed in the afternoon.

July 18 Sabbeth

A beautiful day. Went to church. Here Mr Cob lecture in the session house. The second hymn that was sung was Jesus loveer of my soul[55] a hymn I love so much I alway's shed tears when I sing it. It seems to express my feelings so much, and I love to sing it but I was so full I had to omit some lines. I could not sing for tears checked my utterances and I could not go on part of the time but I sung it through. The gentlemen all set facing me. I do not know what they thought I was crying about but my feelings are so tender and the second line made me almost burst in tears. I do want to go to Jesus so much. There is nothing I want so much as a sweet rest on Jesus breast a rest from all of earth. My Fathers beautiful earth so splendid for sinful mortals but that heavenly land where Jesus is must be so glorious, who could help wanting a place there at Jesus feet. My little girls and me spent the night alone.

July 19 Monday

Elmira came and washed and I sewed some on the childrens dresses and after sun set my little girls and me had a splendid ride in the buggy.[56] We drove the horses our selves and it was the most eleghant night I ever saw. We called at four of our nabors and was home by nine oclock.

July 20 Tuesday

A dull rainy morning. I sewed the most of the day on the dresses. Received a letter from my dear husband in the evening. It is to bad to have him away from home, but God is our helper. His eyes nether slumber nor sleep. How safe we are in his loving arms. No haven can come without his will and will be all for our good and a blessing in disguise what ever happens.

July 21 Wednesday

A dull rainy morning. Clear in the afternoon. The blacksmith helped Elwood get in hay. Took tea with Elwood. I sewed part of the day on Lizzie dress. A very splendid moonlight night. Gods beautiful sky so clear and bright.

---

[55] Sarah quotes a popular hymn by Charles Wesley first published in 1740. It was included as hymn # 359, "Jesus, lover of my soul" in the *Psalms and Hymns, Adapted to Social, Private, and Public Worship in the Presbyterian Church* (Philadelphia: Presbyterian Board of Publication, 1843), the hymnal in use at the Old Tennent Church at the time. The second line that so moved Sarah reads: "Let me to Thy bosom fly." Sarah was fond of hymn singing and frequently included lines of hymns in her diary.

[56] Buggy: a light one-horse vehicle for one or two people, usually with four wheels.

July 22 Thursday

A very cool splendid day. Arose early. Swept the citchen floor, fed turkeys & chickens. Got breackfast. Cleared it away. Mixed ten large loves of bread. Churned. Made a rice pudding & three kinds of cake. Got dinner. Cleared it away. Cleaned the citchen windows. Went with Elwood a huckel berrying picked about four quarts. Came home. Fed turkeys & chickens. Got supper. Put away clean clothes. Wrote in my diary. Elmira went home in the morning to pick huckleberries. Lizzie helped Elwood take worms off the potatoes & flora picked seed peas and shelled them.

Sarah Tabitha Reid formerly Sarah Tabitha Appelton[57]

July 23 friday

A very beautiful day. Elmira came about eleven oclock and Mr [Plum?] came soon after with a sewing machine. Miss Spencer gave me lessons.[58]

July 24 Saturday

Very busy in the morning. A very nice day. Garret Conover and his sister Kate [59] spent the afternoon. I was very much pleased to see them. Kate is a lovely girl and loves the saviour so much I hope. I finished flora's dress a bout eleven oclock at night and churned in the evening after tea. It was a splendid night.

July 25 Sabbeth

A very eleghant day. I staid home and got dinner and Elmira went to church with Elwood and Lizzie. I went to sabbeth school in the afternoon, and Mr Cobs Eleghant house was burned while he was preaching his afternoon sermon. Set fire by his hired girl with shavens in the stove. The most wonderful Providence I ever knew. I am so very sorry for him. All the church records burnt.[60]

---

[57] Occasionally Sarah signed her entries. This is the only time she included her full maiden name.

[58] The foot-pedaled sewing machine was rapidly becoming a housewife's necessity. Called the "Queen of Inventions" by Godey's Ladies Book, it dramatically reduced the number of hours spent sewing the family's clothing. By the 1870s there were numerous makes of machines on the market at reasonable cost. Sewing machines could be bought on time, and some companies offered trade-in allowances for old machines. Stores in Freehold advertised the Aetna, the Wheeler and Wilson, and the Singer machines.

[59] Garret (18) and Kate (28) Conover lived in Manalapan and were the children of Garret and Theresa Conover, possibly kin of William Reid.

[60] Dr. Archibald Cobb and his wife bought what was known as the "Roy Parsonage" in 1867, remodeling and enlarging it substantially. It had hardly been completed when a fire on July 25, 1869 destroyed it completely. The Monmouth Democrat of July 29, 1869 reported that the fire had started either in the kitchen stove or chimney and the loss totaled $25,000. Rev. Cobb's valuable library, his wife's family portraits, and the sessional records of the Old Tennent Church were also destroyed. The Cobbs soon built a new house nearby.

July 26 Monday

A rainy morning. I was sewing on florra & Lizzies pink calico dres.

July 27 tuesday

A dull morning. Churned and done house work. Sewed some on the machine.

July 28 wednesday

A very beautiful day. Commenced a linen pair of pants for Elwood and at half past ten Conover came for me to go home with him to nurse up Tillie. She is worked down sick. She has four little children two of them twins. She has but very little rest day or night. I went with him and staid until friday night. He brought me home.

July 29 thursday

A fine day. A little dull in the morning. Waited on tillie and three little children. Took me nearly all the time. Sewed a little in the afternoon with one of the twins on my lap. Tillie is a gaining slowly.

July 30 friday

A splendid day. Very busy. A good job to wait on two babes although they are very good. Ironed some in the afternoon. Came away about four in the afternoon. Had a splendid ride. Found all well at home. Mrs Preston[61] went home with Con.

July 31 Saturday

Very busy doing house work and fixing every thing in order and thingss nice to eat for my Dear husband. He has been away four weeks and we shall be so glad to see him home. Had five hands helping get in the oats with Elwood. Have a splendid lot of oats. Finished florries dress in the afternoon. The children went with Elly to the station to see their Father in the afternoon. Miss Kate Perine called with Miss Buck.[62] Mr Reid came at six oclock.

July 31 [August 1] Sabbeth[63]

Went with Mr Reid to see Tillie. Wanted so much to stay with her two or

[61] Elizabeth (Conover) Preston: the mother of Sarah's son-in-law

[62] Miss Buck: probably a member of the Buck family who were nearby neighbors on the main road to Freehold.

[63] Sarah sometimes confused the dates and days of the week of her entries. Here, for some reason, she adds a second July 31 for her Sunday entry. Because August 1 fell on Sunday in 1869, all Sarah's dates for August are incorrect. [Correct dates have been inserted in brackets]

three days but Mr Reid could not spare me from home. He will be home such a short time and came home in the evening.

August 1 [2] Monday

A beautiful day. Washed and baked some and sewed on the machine, and fixed to go to the branch [Long Branch] on the morrow.

August 2 [3] Tuesday

Arose early and started when we was ready about eight oclock. We had a splendid ride. Was there half past two. Eat our dinner and went in to bathe. Had a nice time in the water. Then took a splendid ride through Mr Hoe's park.[64] Had a splendid ride home. Was not tired. Made the fire and got tea. Iron Mr Reid a shirt. After tea read a chapter and said my prayers and went to bed. Rode 32 miles besides our pleasure trip. Our horses was just as keen as when we started. We drove Patchen my Jennie Lyn my pet horse.[65] She has been mine ever since she was a colt.

August 3 [4] Wednesday

A beautiful day. Arose very early and ironed some clothes for Mr Reid. He went to new york in the eight oclock train. Lizzie and Florra drove the horses back three miles and came safe home.[66] Elmira went home.

How wonderful is Gods goodness to us. I was lost in wonder love and Jesus when I think how wonderful is his goodness and kind care. Tears will always start when I think of his tender love. He says they may forget yet will I never forget thee.

He has been always around and about my path and has kept me in all my ways that my footsteps shoud not slip and he will be my guide even until death.

> Oh for a heart to prais my God
> A heart from sin set free
> A heart that always feels thy blood
> So freely shed for me.
>
> Oh for a heart submissive meek
> My dear Redeemer Throne where only

[64] Holly Wood, the estate of J. Hoey on Cedar Avenue in Long Branch, was an extensive formal garden with statuary, tree-lined alleys, and fountains.

[65] Sarah's "patchen" horse may have been a horse bred by George Pilgrim Patchen, a well-known breeder who periodically offered horses for sale in the area.

[66] This is the first mention of Lizzie driving the carriage. She would be 12 in October, apparently old enough to be entrusted with the responsibility.

Hoey's Park, Long Branch, circa 1870, photograph by G.W. Pach. MCHA Library and Archives, Collection 84 The George H. Moss Jr. Stereograph Collection

Christ is heard to speak
And Jesus reigns alone.[67]

August 4 [5] Thursday

A nice day. Wanted to go to Tillies but did not get off. Was disapointed. Picked peas in the afternoon.

August 5 [6] friday

A showery day. Baked in the morning. Went with the children to Tillies in the afternoon. Came back in the evening. Was out in the shower. Left Lizzie

---

[67] One of the most frequently quoted hymns in Sarah's diary, "Oh For a Heart to Praise my God" by Charles Wesley and first published in 1742. It appeared as hymn #115 in *Psalms and Hymns, Adapted to Social, Private, and Public Worship in the Presbyterian Church* (Philadelphia: Presbyterian Board of Publication, 1843), the hymnal in use at the Old Tennent Church at the time. Sarah misquotes the second verse which reads: "A heart resigned, submissive, meek,/ My great Redeemer's throne,–/ Where only Christ is heard to speak, /Where Jesus reigns alone...."

with Tillie to help her and could hardly do without her. Flora and me was alone until morning, when Elwood got home.

August 6 [7] Saturday

A showery day. Very busy. Went with Elwood to freehold in the afternoon. Called to see Mrs Sheriff Conover.[68] Had a nice time.

August 7 [8] Sabbeth

Went in the morning. We went to the old church. A very eleghant day. Called after church to see James Rue.[69] He is so very sick with Typhoid fever and so young. I am affraid he will never be well and his Mother has met with such a dredful loss. Her husband she grieves so much for him but he is better off. I can-

---

[68] Matilda (Reid) Conover: Sarah's sister-in-law and the wife of Samuel Conover, who had been sheriff of Monmouth country from 1847 to 1850 and again from 1856 to 1859. In 1869 Samuel Conover was a Freeholder for the Township of Freehold.

[69] James Rue: the son of Lewis Rue, a Manalapan farmer. The Rues lived on the Englishtown Turnpike not far from the Old Tennent Church.

not grieve for friend that I have reason to believe has a place at Jesus feet a place I covet so much. Will I reach that happy place where Jesus is.

August 8 [9] Monday 1869

A pleasant day. Flora and me all alone the most of the night. Sewed on the machine some and fixed to bake in the afternoon. Miss Lizzie Perine called.

August 9 [10] Tuesday

A splendid day. Tillie and her four little children and husband came. We had a nice time. I took care of little willie in the night. I bed him three times in the night and got him asleep every. I did not sleep much but how poor Tillie gets any rest I cannot think.

August 10 [11] Wednesday

A beautiful day. I went in the afternoon with my son and son in law to camp meeting.[70] Had a splendid time. Saw Miss Mary Hankerson[71] and the widow of the Rev. Mr. Armes.[72] Had not seen her since I was a very little girl.

Tillie went home in the evening with his little ones, and took Lizzie with her and I do miss her help so much.

August 11 [12] Thursday

A very beautiful day. Churned in the morning and done house work.

August 12 [13] Friday

Ironed in the morning and sewed in the afternoon. Aunt Margaret took tea with me. Had a nice time. Very tired. Done this weeks Ironing in the morning.

August 13 [14] Saturday

A very splendid cool day. Elwood went to the branch [Long Branch] to take a wash in the Atlantic Ocean and did not get home until near morning and me and little Flora was all alone. I am so tired of being alone at night. I hope something will turn up to oblige me a little. I whitewashed the citchen in the morning and Elmira cleaned the floor.

---

[70] Camp meetings were popular religious revivals held out of doors or under tents for several days during the summer months.

[71] Probably Mary D. Hankinson: an older, single woman who owned her own home in Englishtown.

[72] Sarah Woodhull (Forman) Armes (1808-1872): the widow of Clifford Smith Armes (sometimes spelled Arms), a 1827 graduate of the Princeton Theological Seminary. Armes was the minister of the Presbyterian Church of Madison, NJ from 1832 to 1851. Thereafter he served a church in Ridgebury, New York until his death in 1863. Sarah was the granddaughter of the Rev. John Woodhull of Freehold.

August 14 [15] Sabbeth

A very warm day. Did not go to church. Elwood did not feel very well. John Hendricks called in the afternoon to see Elwood and Cab Reid. I went over to uncle Johny Jewells but did not set down. It was late and Elwood wanted to go away. Had a walk in the peach orchard.

August 15 [16] Monday

A very nice day. Elmira came and washed. I sewed a little on the sewing machine.

August 16 [17] Tuesday

Elmire ironed some and I baked and done the housework.

August 19 [18] Wednesday

Nice day. Churned in the morning and went to freehold and bought Flora a pair of shews. Paid three dollars for them and bought me a [shelby?] calico dress.

August 20 [19] Thursday

A nice day. I ironed in the morning. Elwood went to camp meeting in the afternoon. Elmira called. I paid her two dollars. Elwood did not get home until near morning. It was one of the sweetest moonlights nights I ever saw and I was affraid to stay alone with flora although I know God is my keeper and has always been around my path to keep me in the way. I feel sometimes as if angels must have been set to keep guard arround me so peaceful and safe has been my path through this world of dangers and snares. I can never prais God enough for his many mercies.

August 21 [20] friday

Our horses went to the branch [Long Branch] to take Charly Gravat and Elmira. The warmest day of the summer and so dusty. Aunt Margaret & uncle Bennie spent the afternoon with me and fetched me a basket of peaches. We had a very nice time. We made ice cream and it was very good. Such a warm day.

August 23 [21] Saturday

Oh such a warm morning I never felt when I had all my work to do. I thought I nevey could get breckfast. I felt so weak. It was hard work and the citchen so warm I went down seller to churn and put ice in the churn and the presperation pored off my face all the time in the seller. I was completely out done. I swept the chamber and set down to make me a cape and finished it about four oclock and felt so uneasy about my husband for fear he was out in the sun at work. It was not fit for any one to work in the sun. We had a very sweet shower about five oclock and I never was more glad of rain. My flowers and every thing else is almost dead.

August 23 [22] Sabbeth

A dull looking morning. I wanted to go and hear Mr Cob preach but had no one to stay and keep house and so I had to stay but God is every where. I am so thankful that he is a God every where he can hear our feeblest call. It is a splendid moonlight night and I am all alone with two little children and such a coward as I am. Charly Foster came this morning.

August 24 [23] Monday

A very splendid day. Elmira came in the morning about half past nine. Elwood and me started for Tillie about ten oclock. Went to Lewis Rues[73] and then to englishtown to Mary Claytons[74]. From there to the dye neighborhood to Tillies.[75] I arived there before one oclock. Found them all well. Had a nice time. Started for home about seven oclock. Home safe before nine. Stoped to garrets store. Joseph Deniece was sick. Stoped to the mill[76] and got some flower [flour].

August 25 [24] Tuesday

A very nice day. Johny Reid was here to tea and Ely Reid [77] called with his wife and three children and Lizzie Clayton. I was very glad to see them. Lizzie is such a sweet turned girl.[78] I baked in the morning and Elmira washed. I made Lizzie a cape to her dress in the afternoon and evening.

August 26 [25] Wednesday

A lovely cool day. Made Flora a bow to her dress and Lizzies. Ironed some. Sewed on Mr Reids shirts in the afternoon.

Elwood and Flora went to Mr. Worlds church[79] to the harvest home[80] about eleven oclock and I took a real long walk about six oclock after my turkeys.

---

[73] Lewis Rue: a Manalapan farmer.

[74] Mary (Reid) Clayton: William Reid's younger sister.

[75] Sarah's route gives a clue to the location of Tillie and Conover Preston's home. Several homes in Englishtown were owned by the Dey family. Sarah implies Tillie lived in this area, approximately a two-hour buggy ride from her home.

[76] Sarah probably stopped at the grist and saw mill on the Manalapan River known as the Oakland Mills.

[77] Ely Reid: William Reid's nephew, the son of his eldest brother James and his wife, Mary (Ely) Reid.

[78] A girl with a sweet disposition.

[79] Mr. World's church: the Rev. Charles Flavel Worrell (1805-1881) had, until recently, been the minister of the Presbyterian church in Perrineville.

[80] The harvest home was a fund-raising and social festival in many churches. The Old Tennent Church began its harvest home tradition in 1868 as a June strawberry festival.

August 27 [26] Thursday

A very pleasant day. Set down and commenced some shirts for Mr Reid. In the afternoon I had the pleasure of seeing Miss Ella Debois and sister Julia and Miss Kate Perine and I enjoyed their company very much. They spent the afternoon with me. Mr Debois came for them in the evening.

August 28 [27] Friday

A very nice day. Finished Mr Reid a shirt and commenced another. Worked hard to get it done but did not. Goodness and mercy still surrounds my path and my lying down, for thou art acquainted with all my ways. Oh what a comfort to know that our Merciful God sees and knows all my thoughts. I rejoice so much that God knows all my way's. He knows how I have tryed to shun the very appearance of evil, and how hard I have tried to bear all my little trials of life meekly for his sake who bore so much for me. My motto has always been whosoever smiteth thee on thy right cheek turn to him the other also.

August 29 [28] Saturday

A very nice day. Baked in the morning and finished Mr Reid a shirt. Made pies two cakes sponge and cream cakes and a pudding and fixed for company. Mr Reid came in the five oclock train with Mr Nettleton to buy our patchen horse that I liked so much. Mr Reid gave her to me when she was a colt and I could drive her so nice. I felt so sorry to have her sold. He took her away on monday morning before light. We saw a star on the twenty first of the month if I recollect right which seemed to be in a blaze. A streak of light arose from it a distance and then grew smaller and appeared as though the wind wafted it slowly towards the south. It was getting dusk and we watched it for some time until it was cuite dim. It grew paler and paler until lost to sight.[81]

August 30 [29] Sabbeth

A beautiful day. Mr Reid Mr Nettleton and Elwood went to church and Elmira went home. I had the mornings work to do up with Flora help and dinner to get. Con and Tillie and children came to see their Father and Garet Deniece & Virginia also folow. They came from church. I had a large table full and got tea for them before they went home. Had a bad head ache all night. Could not sleep and was so tired I could not lay still.

August thirtieth first [30] Monday

A very nice day. Patchen went away. I mended some and done the house

---

[81] What Sarah saw in the sky cannot be identified for certain. Perhaps it was a meteor, perhaps a brilliant planet slowly sinking below the horizon.

work in the afternoon. Went with Mr Reid to freehold and took tea at his sister Matilda's.[82] Had a very pleasant time. Came home about dusk.

Sep 1 [August 31] Tuesday

Arose early. Ironed some shirts for Mr Reid. He went to newyork in the eight oclock train. I am so sorry to have him go. I am so much affraid he will get sick or some thing will happen to him. He is a good kind husband and Father. I baked nine large loves of bread a pudding and a cake, pealed pears and pickled fourteen. Cleared away the dinner work. Cleaned two messes[83] of sea bass. Went in the [. . .] and gathered sweet corn and cut it off and put an oven full in the oven to dry. Got tea. Fed the chickens. Cleared tea away with Lizzies help. Lizzie and Elmira went away before noon. Leander Jewll[84] called and Charly Jemason in Afternoon. Rote in my diary. Read some in the bible. Made a prayer and went to bed. Had a good nights rest.

I think so often of that land of rest where sweet rest will never end. Oh I long to have the river pased and reach the other side where Jesus is, but my heart is so cold and incencible.

Oh for a heart to praise my God a heart from sin set free that always feels thy blood so freely shed for me.

A heart resigned submissive meek
My dear redeemers throne
Where only God is heard to speak
Where Jesus reigns alone.[85]

Sep 2 [1] Wednesday

A splendid cool day. I got breckfast and churned. Caned peaches. Helped get dinner and helped Elmira clear it away. She came about ten oclock and ironed some in the afternoon. I helped get tea and cleared it away. Picked some beans and sewed some in the afternoon. The egg man came and paid me ten dollars one of wich was Elwoods.[86]

Sep 3 [2] Thursday

A splendid cool day. I swept the yard and some other jobs. Lizzie and me

---

[82] Matilda (Reid) Conover: William Reid's younger sister.

[83] Mess: a haul or take of fish.

[84] Leander Jewell: the 21-year-old son of Sarah's cousin, William Henry Jewell and his first wife Rebecca (Reid) Jewell. Leander is listed as a wheelwright in the 1870 U. S. Census. Later he opened a harness making and upholstery shop in West Freehold.

[85] This is the second verse of Sarah's favorite hymn: "O! For a Heart to Praise my God."

[86] Keeping poultry was the domain of the farm wife, and the sale of eggs was an important source of income.

walked over to uncle Johneys Jewell and spent the day. We had a very nice time. They had company in the afternoon Mrs David Reid[87] and Miss Pippenger[88] & Henry Jewell & wife[89] & Charly Jemison. I was very glad to see them. I had happy time all so lively and well. Walked home, uncle Johny came with us almost home. Lizzie Armstrong[90] was buried to day.

Sep 3 Friday

A beautiful cool morning. All well. God is good to us His mercy never fails. It is like the great deep so wonderful we cannot comprehend it.

Went to freehold in the afternoon. Called to Mrs. Hendricksons. A very pleasant call. Called on Mr Monroe the flower man to see how to take care of my orange coloured lilly. Bought a pair of nice blankets. Called on aunt margaret. Came home about sunset. Had a splendid ride. Drove rough and ready and jenny.[91]

Sep 4 Saturday

Pleasant day. All well. Elly went to Tillies in the afternoon. Lizzie and me went to aunt Margarets in the morning. Spent the day with her very pleasantly. Saw uncle Gilberts folks.[92]

Sep 5 Sabbeth

A splendid Sabbeth morning. Went with Elwood church at Manalapan and he invited the freinds to Miss Robisons[93] funeral. Came home by the Depot to invite Mr Davis[94] family and took dinner to uncle Gils. When we came home we had a company of young men to see Elwood. They was his cousins. They staid a short time and then I was all alone with Lizzie and our Duchman just from Germany.[95] I did not like to stay much.

Sep 7 [6] Monday

Pretty busy in the morning. Went in the afternoon to uncle Gills and fetched

[87] Mary Ann Reid: the wife of David Reid, a distant relative of Sarah and William from whom they bought much of their farm land. The David Reids lived nearby in Manalapan.

[88] Probably a member of the nearby Pittenger family.

[89] William Henry Jewell: Sarah's cousin and the son of John and Harriet Jewell: his wife was Martha (Jemison) Jewell.

[90] Elizabeth Armstrong: the 22 year-old daughter of William Armstrong of Freehold who died on August 30, 1869.

[91] The horses.

[92] Gilbert Applegate: Sarah's uncle by marriage, the husband of her maternal aunt, Susan (Reid). The Applegates lived in Englishtown.

[93] Ella E. Robinson, daughter of Matilda Robinson, died in Freehold on September 4, 1869 at the age of 18.

[94] Davis was the proprietor of a store at the Englishtown train station.

[95] Sarah uses the term "Duch" (Dutch) for German speakers. Itinerant workers and vagrants frequently stopped at the farm, some of whom made Sarah fearful.

Hatty[96] home with me. Received a letter from my husband. It rained a little and we did not get home until after dark. All safe and Gods goodness around us.

Sep 8 [7] Tuesday

A very splendid day. Very busy canning peaches. Canned 14 cans and baked in the morning bread and cake and a pudding. About half past nine in the morning Mr Combs brought Mrs Armes I was very glad to see her. She is such a good woman and one that has not a great deal of this worlds goods and so she was doubly welcome. She helped me with my peaches. Spent a very happy day. Elmira washed.

Sep 9 [8] Wednesday

A very beautiful morning. Very busy churning and cooking peaches. Elmira sick. Could not or did not want to help do any thing. About eleven oclock Con came for me. His little Joe was sick. Had a spasm in the morning. I did not know how to go but his mother had company and could not go, and I had Mrs. Arms and Elmira sick and so much work to do but if his own mother sent him off without assistance I could not. I went and left all. Mrs Arms cooked my peaches and Lizzie done the work with Mrs. Arms assistance and the duchman finished the churning. All went very well but they forgot the peaches drying in the stove and burned them nearly up. I set up with the sick babe and done every thing I could. I fed it every few minutes through the night but it kept so low that I thought every hour would be its last. Mrs Preston came but could not stay until after twelve which I supposed would be the last hour but it was no worse until morning. It lay just the same. It rained a little in the night.

Sep 10 [9] Thursday

A nice day. I came home in the forenoon. Arived just as they was getting dinner. Found Elmira better. I canned tomatoes and done house work. We had a nice time singing. Mrs Arms led the family worship. It was a great relief to me and I enjoyed it very much. She tried to teach the duchman to serve God. Very splendid moonlight.

Sep 11 [10] Friday

A very nice day. Done house work and cooked peaches and tomatoes. Sewed a little in the afternoon on Lizzies dress. Mrs Armes helped me. After four oclock did not get much done. Had to get tea myself. Elmira was ironing. Enjoyed a splendid moon light night.

---

[96] Hatty Jewell: the daughter of Sarah's cousin Henry Jewell and his second wife Martha (Jemison)

Sep 12 [11] Saturday

A nice day. Very busy. Done house work and baked some in the stove. Dressed chickens and cooked them for sabbeth dinner. Elmira cleaned the citchen and went home. Hattie Jewell went home in the afternoon before she staid four days. We could hardly spare her. She was such a good girl and so pleasant.

Sep 12 Sabbeth

A very splendid day. Elwood took Mrs. Armes and me to the Tennet church. The first it was opened after it was repaired. Mr Cob preached a very good sermon. In the afternoon they all went to sabbeth school, and I had a sweet time reading a book of Mrs Armes.

Sep 13 Monday

A nice day. I baked. Elmira churned and done some house work & I caned some peaches. Baked bread 10 loves apple pies two kinds of cake.

Sep 14 Tuesday

A very nice day. Elmira washed and I done house work. Sewed some in the afternoon. Mrs. Arms helped me some. Beautiful moonlight nights.

Sep 15 Wednesday

A dull morning. Mrs Arms and all but the duchman went to the fair.[97] Had a nice time. Saw a great many friends and a great many beautiful things. Saw a bed spread made of worsted and silk called the log cabben.[98] Very beautiful. I want very much to make one like it. Mrs Arms did not come home with me. She went home with Mr. Andrew Perine. I came home made ready supper in a hurry and went to bed. Elly did not get home very early.

Sep 16 Thursday

A nice day. Churned and washed some clothes and done house work with my little childrens help. Very busy. Caned peaches.
Sarah T Reid daughter
of Sarah Larrance Reid[99]

---

[97] The sixteenth annual Monmouth Country Fair was held on September 14-16, 1869 in Freehold, sponsored by the Monmouth County Agricultural Society. Extensive displays of women's art, handiwork, baked goods, and preserves were among the exhibits.

[98] The log cabin pattern was, and still is, a popular patchwork quilt design.

[99] Sarah Lawrence (Reid) Appleton (1794-1820)

Sep 17 friday

Rained very hard in the morning. I ironed a very large ironing in the morning. The children done the house work. I got tea ready and herd my husbands voice out doors. The storm in the morning had sent him home. Very glad to see him safe home once more. Oh the Lords goodness is always around and about my path and my lying down and art acquanted with all my ways. Oh how I rejoice that he is just such a God so wonderful in goodness mercy and truth and his ways so unreachable and judgements past finding out, but I am satisfied to be passive in his hands and know no will but his. If I had a thousand hearts I would give them all to him and they could never tel or know the half of his <u>goodness</u>.

Oh for a thousand tongs to sing & [. . .]

Sep 18 Saturday

Nice day. Mr Reid got me oven wood and I baked bread and cake, caned peaches for Tillie and churned. The children done the housework. Mr Reid and me started for tillies in the afternoon. Stoped to uncle johny, and got tillie a basket of peaches. Paid one dollar for it a present for tillie. Brought a few of thim home for the children. Stoped to Mrs Vanderveres[100] and got a blue double larkspur a pressent I wanted so much. Got to tillies almost five oclock. Found the babe better but very thin and tillie looked better. Had a nice time. Wanted to come home in the evening but Mr Reid did not want to come and so I had to give in as usual.

Sep 19 Sabbeth

A very nice day. Came home from Tillies very early. Got home a quarter before eight oclock. Fixed for church and went. It was communion and we had an addition of six to our communion. We had a very lovely sermon and I enjoyed it very much. Oh to live near to God to be swallowed up of God and heaven, to behold the brightness of the saviours face and the beams of rapture that fill the heart to overflowing, and the streams of brightness that almost make us forget we are still on the earth, so near the pearly gates that the rapture and glory float through in a clear bright streak of glory from the throne. We wonder the bright beautiful things of earth grow dim and insignificant & the little trials of earth seem small and of no account when compared with our great reward. Well may we count all things but loss for the exictance of the knolledge of Christ Jesus my Lord. No wonder all our enemies and all the prowess of earth sem but as air to waft and help us heavenward. Sure we may smile at satans rage and face a frowning world.

---

[100] Henry J. Van Derveer ran a fruit farm where he sold fruits and plants of many sorts. The Van Derveers lived off the main road to Freehold.

Sep 20 Monday

Arose very early and helped Mr Reid get ready for newyork. Ironed some. Caned tomatoes and worked hard all day. Churned likewise.

Sep 21 Tuesday

Nice day. Caned tomatoes and peaches and very busy. Very tired. Wanted rest so much but had to keep at work trying to sew after I was done housework.

Sep 22 wednesday

Nice day. Very busy baking and churning. Was very tired all day. Hard work to keep to work in the afternoon. About three oclock I set down to sew but so very tired I did not sew long before my lungs was in a great heat and I could hardly get my breath, and could not speak but with great difficulty. I was completely worked sick.[101] I was so anxious to do all I could for my dear ones and my husband has to work so hard to get along. I hope he may have a bright reward in that Glorious home in the skies for his goodness to his dear ones.

God has been so good to me. He has always raised me up friends when I have needed them, & strewed my path with the sweetest roses. Goodness has crowned my days with the brightest beauties of earth.

Sep 23 Thursday 1869

A very beautiful day. Slept but little through the [. . .] feel very weak and no strength to speak. Lungs very weak. Elwood went in the morning for Elmira and she could not come & likewise for Matilda Paterson & she could not come and I was not able to do any things. I am sick. My two little girls done the work and nursed me as good as they could and was very kind to me. I felt better towards night. Aunt Margaret called & Edith in the afternoon.

Sep 24 friday

A little better. A beautiful day. Elmira came in the morning. Worked quite smart. Done all she could. Cleaned the citchen. The children done some of the house work and wated on me some. I wrote some in my diary and a letter to my husband.

Sep 25 Saturday

A nice morning. Elmira baked. I mended some stocking. Felt a little better. Lung's very weak, but God so good his mercy never fails. We may be weak and tired and sick but he is the same good kind Father in heaven. Oh for more love to him. Nearer to Thee my God

---

[101] Sarah performed an enormous amount of heavy physical labor. She seems to develop respiratory problems at this time.

nearer to Thee
although it be a cross
that raiseth me.[102]

Sep 26 1869 Sabbeth

A very unpleasant day. The mishionary Mr McChesney [103] and a mishionary
from China preached. It stormed before we was half way to Church but we went
on. Was pretty wet before we got home.

Sep 27 Monday

*Sabbeth evening after prayers my children was so thoughtless that I was deeply
grieved. I had pleaded for their salvation with tears. I spent most of the night praying
for them in the greatest earnestness with many tears.*

Elmira washed. I helped round a little. Very cold blustery day. I felt better.
Sewed some on the childrens pink dresses.

Sep 28 Tuesday

A cool day. Pleasant in the afternoon. I sewed some on the childrens dress.
Felt worse than I did the weak before. Wanted to go to tillies but could not spare
the horses.

Sep 29 Wednesday

A very pleasant day. Sewed on floras dress. Wanted to go to tillies but could
not spare the horses. In the evening tillie and cousin Margret Alice Appelgate[104]
came with her twins with tillies twin babies and they cried the most of the
night. We did not rest much.

Sep 30 Thursday

A very splendid day. Went with Tillie home. Was so sorry to leave my little
family but they wanted me to go. I went with her to cut a sack[105] & dress for her.
The babies was sick. The Doc said they had the disentary [dysentery]. I slept but

---

[102] Sarah quotes the first four lines of a hymn by Sarah (Flower) Adams first published in 1841. It was
not included in the hymnal in use at the Old Tennent Church at the time and it is unclear where Sarah
would have learned the hymn. Sarah Adams was an English Unitarian, and as her hymn became popular the essentially Deist wording was changed slightly as it was adapted by other denominations in the
19th century. The accurate wording of the hymn read: "Nearer, my God, to Thee, / Nearer to Thee!/
E'en though it be a cross / That raiseth me...."

[103] Rev. William Edgar McChesney: a local man and an alumnus of the Princeton Theological
Seminary, was ordained to the ministry as an evangelist and assigned to work in Canton, China by the
Board of Foreign Missions on October 5, 1869.

[104] Margaret Applegate: Sarah's cousin, the daughter of Uncle Gilbert and Aunt Susan.

[105] Sack: a loose fitting coat or jacket.

little in the night. Spent much of the time in prayer for my children. Their souls is so precious in my sight. I cannot bear that they should not love the dear saviour in their childhood. Oh I do want them so much to love the saviour. I do hope Jesus will early draw them to himself to love his servise. It is so sweet to feel we are his now and forever safe in Jesus arms from all that can molest or make us affraid.

Oct 1 friday

A nice day. Sewed for Tillie all day. Mrs Rue called in the afternoon. Expected Elwood for me in the eve but he did not come.

Oct 2 Saturday

A nice day. Elwood came in the morning for me and brought Mrs Preston with him.

We had a splendid ride home. Got home about eleven oclock. Found all safe. I helped straight up the house for the sabbeth so I could get off early to church.

Oct 3 Sabbeth

A very rainy morning. I was very much disapointed about going to church. Could not go. Had a good time reading in Dr Elexanders book [Alexander's *Thoughts on Religious Experience*] and learnt flora some questions.

Oct 4 Monday

A stormy day. Elmira did not come. My little daughters done the most of the work and let me sew and mend stockings in the evening. I went down to get tea and soon after my husband came in. I was very glad to see him home safe once more. Oh the goodness of my heavenly father. How thankful I am that his eyes nether slumbers nor sleeps. What would we be without his watchful guardian care so full of goodness and mercy.

Oct 5 Tuesday

Dull morning. Very busy baking. In the afternoon went with Mr Reid to freehold. Called on Mrs Sherref Conover. Took tea with her. She made me a present of some cranberries. Went with Fannie Conover to Mrs Ros's. Got a splendid flower of her. Mr Reid bought a nice buggy and brought it home with us.

Oct 6 wednesday

Splendid day. Went with my husband to make some calls. Called on his sister Mary Clayton. Very pleasant time. Called on Aaram[106] his brother and had a

---

[106] Aaron L. Reid: William Reid's youngest brother.

pressent of some peppers. Very nice time. They have such sweet children. Went
on to his nephews and took dinner Mr Ely Reid and his mother. Very pleasant
visit. Did not stay long. Came on home and Mr Reid went to new york in the
five oclock train. I was very sorry to have him go. Oh it is so hard to see him go
from home to keep his family when his Father had plenty to make all of his children comfortable to get along in the world if he had divided it equally among
them but some of them he has left more than they will ever need.[107] Achsy
Perine took tea with me.

Oct 7 Thursday

A nice day. Sewed on the childrens dresses. Very busy and swept the house
through.

Oct 8 friday

Very splendid day. The fish man came and I bought over one hundred weight.
Mrs Conover came about nine in the morning. I was very glad to see her. She is
a freind I esteem very hily and spent the day. I was invited to Mr Vlets to tea but
could not go. In the afternoon uncle gilbert came with aunt susan. I was very
glad to see them and lilly also. They took tea with me.

Oct 9 Saturday

A nice day. Baked in the morning. Went with the children to see Alice
Quackenbush and she gave me a sutheren rose bush. Went in the evening to
mounts corner to the store.[108]

Oct 10 Sabbeth

A very dull rainy day. Went to church with elwood and flora to church. Mr
Cob preached to the children. It was very nice. We had to drive home like
smoke to escape the rain. Jenny my pet horse was pretty foamy when we got
home. It stormed dredfully all the afternoon. Sweet lovely rain showers of mercy
from above fills our cup to overflowing only we will not always see it.

> Mercy without bottom or shore,
> Debth of mercy can it be
> Mercy face for even me.

Oct 11 Monday

Its cleared off in the morning. Elmira did not come. I mended Mr Reid coat.
Took to Charly jewells in the afternoon. He had left for the station. I was two

---

[107] Sarah's husband was one of twelve children, many of whom, and their children, lived in the area.
Her father-in-law John Reid died in 1868, leaving some of the children better off than others.
[108] Mounts Corner: the main crossroads in West Freehold.

late. I was so sorry for it. Stoped to aunt Margarets and had a nice little stay. So sweet to meet dear ones. Came home and got tea. Elmira came in the evening.

Oct 12 Tuesday

A dull day. Went in the morning to my cousin henrie jewells with flora. Had a nice time. Saw aunt Hariet & aunt Margaret and uncle Bennie and aunt susan and cousin Martha and her little Hatty and her little Lizzie. Called at Mr Davises store. Had a nice time with Mrs Davis. She gave me some slips of her flowers. Drove home pretty smart about six miles for it threatened to rain any minute.

Oct 13 wednesday 1869

All well. Very busy making the childrens dresses.

Oct 14 Thursday

Nice day. Finished lizzies dress and done house work.

Oct 15 friday

Nice day. Baked. Commenced Elwood a black cloth vest. Worked very study on it. Had a headach all day. Rained in the afternoon. Elwood went for the children to the school house.

Oct 16 Saturday

A nice day. I sewed the most of the day on elwoods vest. Finished it in the evening. Had a headache all day. Elmira & Lizzie went in the afternoon to Mr Appelgates. Came home in the evening. Splendid moonlight evening.

Oct 17 Sabbeth

Nice day. Elwood went to perinesvill [Perrineville] to church and I had to stay home from church. I was sorry. Went to drive my turkkeys and took a walk in the afternoon. Went to sabbeth school with Lizzie and Flora. The duchman harnessed the horses and Lizzie drove. Had a splendid time so pleasant. Stoped to charlys to hear from Mr Reid. I am worried a bout him. He has been gone more than a week and no letter from him. Charly was in new york so short a time he did not see him.

Oct 18 Monday 1869

A nice morning. The childr[en] went to school and Elmira did not come and I had so much to do baking bread 11 loves and making cake two kinds and frosting them and cooking and doing housework. In the evening I was worked completely sick. The children came home from school and helped me. Got tea and cleared it away or I could not have finished the days work.

Oct 19 Tuesday

Nice morning. The children went to school. Elmira came in the morning and dressed chickens for me. I was very busy sweeping the yard and fixing the parlor and sitting room and every thing in order for company in the afternoon. It is Lizzies birthday and I have invited her school teacher and school mates to selebrate her twelth birthday. Elwood went to school after them in the rain. They spent the evening and had a splendid time. They all seemed to enjoy it very much and we enjoyed their company very much. The teacher seemed to be a very pleasant girl. Elwood took them home about eleven oclock.

Oct 20 Wednesday

Nice day but cool. Very much worried a bout Mr Reid. Sent to the office. No litter. Could not half work. Done the house work and Elmira washed. Had a bad head ache. Went to bed early but could not sleep splendid moonlight night. Worried all night about Mr Reid. I am so affraid something has happened to him. He always wrote every week and some times twice a week. He went away in the late train and did not get there before nine at night. I am affraid some robber killed him before he reached his bourding house.

Oct 21 Thursday

Sewed in the morning. Mending clothes in the afternoon. Went to the corner for a letter and did not get any. Went to Charly Jewells molases house to see if he was going to newyork. It come on to rain or I would have gone to freehold to telegraphed to new york to see if I could learn anything of Mr Reid. I am worried sick about him. A nephew of mine is sick. Leander Jewell has the billious fever.[109]

Oct 22 Friday

A very cool morning. Went out. Took the children to school and went to freehold and telegraphed to New York to Mrs Kenard[110] to hear if she knew any thing of Mr Reid. I am so much affraid something has happened to him. He never let a week pass without writing to me before and I could not get an answer to day. I went again at four oclock and no answer came. I am so much troubled about him. It is so hard that he must leve his dear ones at home and go to a distant city to make a living for them, and surrounded with so many dangers. My only hope has been in Gods help and mercy and kind care of him*. I could not have rested one week but I know that his watchful eye was upon him, and I hope still Gods is around and about his path and his lieing down and acquainted

---

[109] Leander Jewell had typhoid fever.
[110] Presumably Mrs. Kenard is the landlady where William Reid boarded in New York City.

with all his way's. Oh wonderful goodness for such a Great God to have a care for us who are but dust and ashes.

Oh my Father help me always to prais and adore thee.

I am lost in wonder love and prais when I think of thy greatness and mercy. Oh for a thousand tongues to sing my great dear redeemers prais.

> Oh for a heart to prais my God
> A heart from sin set free
> A heart that always feels thy blood
> So freely shed for me
> Oh my saviour fill me full
> of heaven and thee heaven and thee.[111]

*my husband

Oct 23 Saturday

Cold and stormy. Was so much worried about my husband I could not work. Mended some cloths. Elwood went in the rain to the telegraph office and there was no word for me.

I was worried almost to death about Mr Reid in the afternoon. Elwood went again to the telegraph office, and wated for the five oclock train. Mr Reid came with the train and I was so glad to see him safe home again. The lady he boarded with received the message by telegraph and did not know enough to answer it or was too queer to do it. When Mr Reid came home in the evening he was tired and he made up his mind to come home the next day and was too busy to telegraph in the morning. He knew I had not received his letter and so came home in the afternoon train.

My heart overflows with gratitude to God for his unspeakable goodnes in protecting my husband when surrounded with so many dangers. What great condecencion in him to take knolledge of us.

Oct 24 Sabbeth

A cool morning. Went with Mr Reid to see Tillie. He had not seen her in five weeks. He could not go back without seeing her. Stoped to mrs Prestons and took dinner with them. Con and Tillie was there. Came home and called to see Wilse Hendricksson. He has been almost killed by Mr Eseck Hartshorn and his son James pushed him out of his wagon when his horses was going very fast and

---

[111] Hymn #538 in *Hymnal, Ordered by the General Assembly* (Philadelphia: Presbyterian Board of Publication, 1867). " Lost in wonder, love, and praise" is the last line of the third and final verse of Charles Wesley's familiar hymn "Love Divine, all Love Excelling."

then hit him on the head with a club twice so Hendricksson says his jaw bone is broke in two places and very badly hurt.[112]

Oct 25 Monday

Very cool. Very busy baking and washing. Mr Reid went to Englishtown with his little girls. I could not go I was so busy.

Mr Reid had his girls weighed and Lizzie is twelve years old and weighed one hundred lb and Florra is eight years and eight months[113] and weighed eighty lb. Two very fleshy girls good and helthy. He went to newyork in the three and half train. I am so sorry to have him go from his good comfortable home that he enjoys so much. He is never from home except on business unless I am with him if I am well.

Oct 26 Tuesday

A very splendid day. I commenced to clean the chamber and with Elmira help cleaned three rooms and the hall. Very tired at night.

Oct 27 Wednesday

A very cold morning. I made a fire in my room and cleaned it. I white washed it and cleaned the windows (which is four) and cleaned the wood work, and a hall and Elmira cleaned the floor. I came down and got tea. Set yeast to bake with. Cleared the tea table and churned some. Elwood finished it for me. I took up the butter.[114] Straightened my room and went with Elmira to Mr Appelgates after the children about ten at night, and I was very tired. They ought not to have stayed but I did not schold them. Came home very tired and cold and went to bed.

> Oh for a heart to prais my God
> A heart from sin set free.

Oct 28 Thursday 1869

Dull and stormy. I baked and done house work, nine loves of bread and six pies and a cake. Got dinner. Cleared it away. Got tea and cleared it away. Elmira

---

[112] The assault Sarah refers to occurred on October 22 and was reported in the *Monmouth Democrat*, October 28, 1869 under the headline, "Terrible Affray." The incident occurred when Wilson Hendrickson, a young farmer driving with two young women relatives, stopped by the road on his way to Black's Mills to gather chestnuts on the property of Esek Hartshorne. A dispute ensured that resulted in the near fatal beating of Hendrickson by Esek and his son, James. The newspaper commented: "All the parties in this affray are respectable and wealthy people....By a single burst of passion they have brought shame to their friends, and possibly disgrace to themselves." The Hartshornes were arrested and indicted for assault and battery. They were tried in Freehold, found guilty, and fined $200 on January 31, 1870.

[113] Florence was born in 1862; she was seven years, eight months.

[114] Sarah took the finished butter from the churn.

was ironing. I am so tired I am almost sick to night. I have not for three days set down from morning until night except at meal times. I have done more than my share of the work but if I live tomorrow I shall let some one else do or it will be undun.

It is a very warm dull night not a stir of wind to be felt. I would not ask Lizzie to help me clear the tea away for night before last I asked her to wipe the tea things for Elmira for we was tired and she made a great noise about it and such a time I would rather do them fifty times than have such a noise. What little thanks Mothers receive for all their trouble and care.

Oh my Father help me to do all thy holy will and bear all patiently.

Oct 29 friday

A nice day. Very windy. I am almost sick but I set down to sew on flora dress and worked all day, at some thing.

Oct 30 Saturday

A very cold day. I swept the chamber and mended some. In the afternoon the children came home from school very cold but would not come to the fire although I insisted uppon their warming themselves.

Oct 31 Sabbeth

A cold day. Elwood took Elmira and me to church. We herd Mr McChesney & Mr Marselles[115] make their farewell address before starting for China & Mr Broad Head[116] from India preached the sermon from the words to what purpose is this waist [waste]. A very good sermon, and Mr Lion[117] from Ohio made a good address also. He is very smart. He is going to sail with our missionaries to China on Nov 2nd. At twelve oclock, in the afternoon I went with my two little girls to sabbeth school. Was very late. I have to ride so far to church I could not get there in time. It commenced at two oclock and it was after one to day when we got home. Flora was taken sick in the evening.[118]

Nov 1 Monday

A very cool night. Flora was very sick all night and a hot fever was flity in the morning. Very sick all day and a high fever and soar throat. I worked all day

---

[115] Rev. Algernon Marcellus (1840-1896), an alumnus of the Princeton Theological Seminary, was affiliated with the Presbytery of Canton, China in 1870-71.

[116] Rev. Augustus Brodhead (1831-1887), an alumnus of the Princeton Theological Seminary, served as a missionary in India from 1858-1878.

[117] Rev. David N. Lyon, an alumnus of the Western Theological Seminary, served as a missionary in Hangchow, China from 1870-1880.

[118] Florence probably had developed strep throat. Sarah applied various home remedies hoping to reduce the symptoms.

with her. In the evening she was worse. Did not know any thing for a while. I soaked her feet and put on onion clouths. Mr Bearmorse son went for Dr Vote.[119] He came about nine in the evening and left her medasne [medicine] which relieved her. Her fever went off and she had a good sleep.

Nov 2 Tuesday

Nice day. Flora is better. She could not stay in bed she was so tired of it. I am so glad she is better. I thought last night she would not live she was so bad. She did not know any thing for a short time. I wated on her and baked & sewed on her dress.

Nov 3 Wednesday

Splendid day. I brought Flora down in the sitting room. I was very busy all day doing house work. Elmira was washing. In the evening Johny Reid came to invite Elwood to Spafford Reids[120] wedding. The setting sun was most georgeous in splendor. Gods works is so glorious and grand. How eleghant he has made the earth, even the green grass is so beautiful.

Nov 4 Thursday

A very eleghant. Day we commenced to clean the sitting room. Elwood went about three oclock to the wedding, and soon after Tillie came with her four little ones and drove herself. I was very glad to see her home all well. If we could always keep our children arround us we might enjoy earth so much more, and our anxiety would be so much less.

Nov 5 friday

A very dull morning warm and muggy. I was almost sick. My lungs was soar with work. I am thankful I can work, but I have too much for my strength. I think it will kill me but I do all for the sake of Jesus. He has done so much for me, it makes all I do seem sweet. I have tried so much to bear all patiently for his sake. I have always remembered his words since I was a child which he said, if they smite thee on one cheek turn the other also. I have always left it to God to avenge me when I was wronged and treated evil, and he has turned darkness into light and made crooked things straight. It has been dark rainy and misty but a little before sunset the sun shone out so lovely with such a clear sweet radiance. Oh I thought God will shine so on my last days with such splendor he is able and may his Glory guild with heavenly splendor declining ray. Tillie started

[119] Dr. John Vought (1816-1882), a graduate of the Albany Medical College in 1839, established a practice in Freehold with his uncle, John B. Throckmorton. He had offices on Main Street and practiced for 42 years.

[120] John and Spafford Reid: William Reid's nephews, the sons of John H. Reid, his younger brother. Spafford Reid married Hester E. Burtt on November 4, 1869 at her home in Monroe.

for home about three oclock, and uncle Henry and aunt margaret came just before, to tel me my nephew was no better that lays so low with Typhoid fever Leander Jewell Mr Reids sisters son and son of my cousin Henry Jewell. I have got my husbands letter started for this office this afternoon. I have wrote in it every day this week I believe but could not get Elwood to take it to the office.

Nov 6 Saturday

A very nice day. Done chamber work. Tacked sitting room carpet and washed the out side of windows. Mended clothes in the afternoon. Acksia Perine called in the afternoon and I went part of the way with her home. Read some in the observer [New York Observer].[121] Read a chapter in Gods holy work. Said my prairs. Went to bed. Had a good nites rest.

Nov 7 Sabbeth

A very cold blusterry day. Went to church. Herd Mr Cob preach from the the words of the saviour. Father I will that they whom then hast given me be with me where I am. Precious words of the dear saviours. Oh I can never have him enough for all he has done for me. I want to be filled with love that I can hold no more. Do hear saviour. Fill me full of heaven and thee.

Nov 8 Monday 1869

A nice cold day and very windy. Elwood came home about ten oclock. I got a bad cold getting in wood on sunday eve and this morning I had to go out for chips and got cold. Had a soar throat before night. Sewed most of the day. In the eve Mr Reid came home from new york. I was very glad to see him. It is so cold we need him home so much.

Nov 9 Tuesday

A little warmer in the morning but very pleasant through the day. Most sick with a cold. Baked in the morning. Mr Reid went to new york in the afternoon. I was very sorry to see him go. I set down and commenced a letter to him and Elwood and Lizzie fell out about the horses and she cried herself amost to death. I never seen a child cry so. I was so sorry to see her cry so hard.

---

[121] The New York Observer was one of the important New York journals after the Civil War. It was a well-established non-partisan Protestant newspaper published by Sidney E. Morse Jr. and Co. The paper was originally founded as a Presbyterian paper but by Sarah's time had severed any official ties to the Presbyterian church and disclaimed being the "organ of any religious denomination." It came out weekly on Thursdays and billed itself as the "oldest and Best Family Newspaper." Its editors asserted that "In this age of development and new ideas in religion, as well as in everything else—a character for stability and truthful order is worth something. It is of some importance to know that the paper you read and put in the hands of your family, is not insidiously teaching false doctrine or latitudinarian error."

Nov 10 wednesday

A very nice day. I fixed to bake some nice bread to take with me tomorrow to the church but I have got up with such a head ache and soar throat it is not safe for me to fix and bake and cook chickens. I am too sick I cannot do it. I am very sorry I wanted to go so much to the old church, but I shall not be able. I better sit by the stove and get my cold better. Mended some. In the eve a dutchman came and stay all night.[122] I was so much affraid of him.

Nov 11 Thursday

A splendid sunshiny day. I feel a little better but it is too windy for me to go out. Elwood went to church for the bible society[123] and met Elmira and children went to her uncles and I was alone and the duchman came back. I had the doors locked so he could not get in. He cut some wood. Cab Reid came here about dusk. I am so much affraid the duchman would come back. He came just after Cab came. Elwood came soon after. I got tea and Elmira and the children soon came. Elwood let the duch come in and stay all night. I was very much affraid of him.

Nov 12 friday

A clear nice morning. Elmira was sick and went home. Lizzie was very horse. I put a mustard plaster on her breast.[124] She was better and some bitter weed tea to drink. I had all the work to do and the ironing, and was half sick. Elwood started the dutchman off. I was very tired at night. Went to freehold in the afternoon about four oclock. The children and Elwood kept house. Aunt Margaret went with me. We went to Mis Weeds Milinary store.[125]

Nov 13 Saturday

A cold windy day. Con came down early and helped Elwood kill the beef. Lizzie and flora would be out doors to see them, and I could not get them to help

---

[122] Wayfaring immigrants often passed Sarah's farm looking for odd jobs and a night's shelter. Sarah's fear of the German itinerant may have been prompted by the attempted murder of a Long Branch housewife by an inebriated German employee just a month before. The incident had been reported in the *Monmouth Democrat*, October 21, 1869.

[123] The Old Tennent Church was host to annual meeting of the Monmouth County Bible Society on November 11, 1869. A special railroad excursion was arranged to take people to the meeting and entertainment and several speakers from out-of-town were scheduled.

[124] Mustard plaster was a common home remedy intended for drawing out infection. It was a paste of powdered mustard and rubber, spread on a cloth and applied to the body.

[125] Miss H. Weed: the owner of the Bazaar on Main Street in Freehold opposite the American Hotel. Her store carried a wide range of millinery and fancy goods: bonnets, children's hats, mourning and bridal veils, laces, hosiery, buttons, fringes, worsted goods, hankerchiefs, collars and cuffs, human hair and mohair braids, chemisettes, tooth and nail brushes, sewing silk and cotton for machine and hand, rubber knitting needles, knitting yarn, ladies' merino vests, and hosiery for men.

me. Lizzie made a great time because I wanted her to clean around the stove, so I gave it up and got the dinner myself and let them stay out until they were satisfied.

Nov 14 Sabbeth

A very storm morning. We did not go to church. About ten it looked like clearing and Elwood fixed and went away. Myself and two little girls spent a very pleasant day. We was alone all night until near morning when Elwood came home. I was affraid all night. I will be so glad when my husband gets home for the winter.

Nov 15 Monday

A cool morning. Elmira did not come. I done the work and the children went to school. Spent a very pleasant day alone with Elwood. Mr Shepherd came and got a hind quarter of beef. It weighed one hundred and thirty lb. Elmira came back in the evening.

Nov 16 Tuesday

A cool dull morning. Elwood and myself went to New Brunswick. We had a splendid ride about twenty two or three miles. We got there at half past ten, done some shopping, got the children dresses and two mull[126] one for Elmira. We started for home five minutes after three. Had a nice ride. Drove jenny and rough and ready. When we was this side spotswoods[127] it commenced to snow about four oclock, and then we drove slow. We was affraid the horses would take cold. We was home a bout seven oclock all safe. Lizzie set herself afire and Elmira put it out.[128] Her sleeve was all burnt up.

Nov 17 wensday

A dredful storm. It stormed hard in the night. We laid in bet late. I got up and put things in place and Elmira got breckfast. We set down exactly at nine oclock. Stormed until eleven oclock very hard. It drove in the front door very much. I baked in the morning and sewed some in the afternoon. Elwood went to Cons in the evening on horsback. The sky was very eleghant. Between three and four oclock or four seemed to be clouds of fleecy gold so very eleghant. Oh the mercy and goodness of God so wonderful in goodnes. Who can shew forth half of his prais.

---

[126] Mull: a fine, soft muslin.

[127] Spottswood: a town northwest of Freehold below what is now East Brunswick.

[128] In a home with open fires in the lamps, fireplaces and kitchen, the danger of burns was very real.

Nov 18 Thursday

A pleasant day. Elwood and Flora myself went to church to hear a thanksgiving Sermon. After the sermon we went to uncle Gilberts to take dinner with them. I called to see my nephew Leander Jewell who has been very low with the fever. Was very glad to see him gaining. Saw Albert Appelton my nephew my only brothers son. Was very glad to see him. He is a nice boy and I have not seen him for more than a year. I herd from my brother[129] and family and spent an hour or two very sweetly with dear friend perhaps for the last. If we should never meet again on earth may we meet in that better land.

Nov 19 friday

A nice day. I spent the most of the time sewing on the childrens dresses. Red ones. In the afternoon Edith Anderson[130] called. I knit in the evening. Read some in the observer [*New York Observer*] which I love so much and sung eight or nine hims. Read some in the bible. Had family prayers.

Nov 20 Saturday

A dull morning. Done some house work. Swept and went to mr Crawfords he is dead and went to freehold. Came back. Took tea to aunt Margarets. Called to uncle Johnies. Came home. Got tea for Elwood and Elmira. Knit some sung some. Read some in the observer and bible. Had family prayers and went to bed.

Nov 21 Sabbeth

A nice morning. The children went to Mr Crawfords funeral. Elwood went to church and came back about one in the morning. I staid home and kept house. We spent the day very nicely in ervy way except Lizzie. She commenced in the morning to shine out. She scolded me in the morning before she was out of bed. She was not willing flora should have a pair of her stockings, and after breckfast she called me an old fool three times because I would not let her do something I do not know what but I made up my mind before I got out of bed that nothing should iritate me or make me forget it was Gods holy day so I made the most of the day. In the afternoon read to the children a nice story about a good girl that went to heaven. The sun set was eleghant. The east was one of golden glory as though it must be the gate of heaven.

Nov 22 Monday

Nice day. Elmira washed. I mended Elwood two pair of pants and some other

---

[129] Sarah's brother James Appleton. She suggests here that she rarely saw him and expected to be parted from him.

[130] Edith Anderson: a servant in the household of Sarah's uncle and aunt, Benjamin and Margaret Van Cleve.

things. Sewed on their dresses. Wrote to Mr Reid in the evening. Samuel Davison called in the evening.

Nov 23 Tuesday

Rained hard in the night. Stormy all day. I mad a new bed tick and filled it with feathers. Worked hard. Mrs Appelgate called & Charly Gravat in the evening.

Nov 24 Wednesday

A wet rainy day. The children was home from school and sewed on their canton flannel drawers.[131] I made the wastes of their dresses and mended some clothes.

Nov 25 Thursday

A splendid cool morning. The children went to school. I was very busy baking. Worked hard. Done the house work and baked bread pies and cake. Elmira was until nearly three oclock renching[132] up cloths. Kate Perine called in the afternoon and brought us an invitation to Lizzies wedding. She is going to marry Mr Taylor.[133] In the evening I wrote to mr Reid.

Nov 26 friday

A nice morning. Aunt margaret came in the morning and took dinner with me. In the afternoon Elwood and myself went to freehold. I got my velvet hat and looked at the Etna [Aetna] sewing machine. Liked it very much. Elwood fetched home the buggy.

Nov 27 Saturday

A dull morning. Swept the chamber and cut out a shirt for Elwood and sewed on it. Mended El[wood's] over coat. Done the cooking. Mended stocking. In the evening read some in the observer and helped Flora learn her geography.

Nov 28 Sabbeth

A cool dull morning. Went to church with Elwood. Herd Mr Cob preach a good sermon very impressive. There had been two funerals through the week, one was the Rev Daniel Maclain[114] for many years the pastor of the tennet

---

[131] Canton flannel: cotton flannel, a common fabric for winter underwear.

[132] Renching: an obsolete or dialect form of the verb to rinse, to wash in clean water.

[133] James A. Taylor of Holmdel Township.

[114] Rev. Daniel Veach McLean (1801-1869), a 1830 graduate of the Princeton Theological Seminary, was minister of the Old Tennent Church from 1832-1836 and of the Presbyterian Church in Freehold from 1838-1850. He received an honorary Doctor of Divinity from Lafayette College in 1848 and served as president of the college from 1851-1857. During much of that time he was also a director of

church also an aged elder Dr John Woodhull.[115] The two men brought from a distanse to be buryed there in one week and they had not been very good friends in their lives time. I thought how singular that God should fetch them so near in death. When they meet in the heavenly world they will not think of their falling out here. Altogether it was very solumn. I was acquainted with both of them when I was a little girl and a year and a half ago Mr Maclain wrode with us to Garret Conovers. I had a very pleasant conversation with him. He was a very smart man. Had a good strong head. A good sound man but a little wordly in his ways. My feelings was very tender. I shed tears several times through the sermon. To do the best I could I could not keep my eyes dry. In the afternoon Lizzie kicked Flora on the side of her nose and hurt her very much. It is dredfully brused. I was very sorry. If she had hit her on the nose it would have broken it. In the evening we read about Jesus raising Lazerus from the dead, and sung several hyms. Wrote some to Mr Reid. I had two nephews to take dinner with me. One was Ely Reid and Johny Reid John Reid son.

Nov 30 [29] Monday

Nice day. Elmira washed. I done the house work and finished Elwood shirt. Sew on flora drawrs in the evening. I had some sweet thought of Gods goodness. In the morning when I awoke I thought how wonderful good God was.

My life has all been mingled with so much of the sweetness of earth and joys of heaven. I can see so plain that Gods hand has warded off all evil. All the darts and trials that Ive met seems to fall harmless at my feet. Nothing seems to affect me. All the little trials of life an unseen hand seems to keep off. I think I feel like Pall [Paul]. I count all but loss for the exelencies of the knolledge of Christ Jesus my Lord. I think nothing two great to bear if I may win heaven at last and have a place at Jesus feet.

Nov 30 Tuesday

A rainy day. Elwood and myself went to see Tillie. Had a nice ride. Found them all well. Took dinner with them. They was very glad to see me especily the children. Came back in the evening. Had a very pleasant ride.

Dec 1 Wednesday

Elmira renched up her clothes. Took her most all day. I done part of the

the Princeton Theological Seminary (1848-1860). At the time of his death he was serving as the pastor of the Presbyterian Church in Red Bank.

[115] Dr. John T. Woodhull (1786-1869): a graduate of the Medical College of Philadelphia where he was a student of Dr. Benjamin Rush; he was the son of Rev. John Woodhull, D.D. Dr. Woodhull had been active in the musical aspects of worship at the Old Tennent Church. In 1824 he was made a clerk "to raise & Carry the sacred musick in the church;" later he was a precentor, one of the men who lined out the hymns for congregational singing. During the pastorate of the Rev. Luther H. Van Doren, Woodhull organized the first church choir and served as chorister.

house work and riped up my purple empress cloth and gored the skirt.[136] Finish two pair of drawrs for the children. The sun set most eleghant. Part of the west was flooded with golden glory. Oh so splendid words can not portray the splendor.

Dec 2 Thursday

Very busy baking bread pies and cake. Got dinner. Nice morning. Snowed in the afternoon. Sewed a little on my dress, and done up the tea things.

Dec 3 friday 1869

Dull morning. Snowed in the night. Elwood went a gunning. Altered a dress. Mrs Perine called and got some butter and engaged cream for the wedding to make ice cream. I finished Floras drawers in the evening.

Dec 4 Saturday

Nice day. Cold in the morning. Very busy doing house work. Sewed some in the afternoon. Mr Reid came home in the afternoon.[137] He had pressents for all. We was so glad to see him safe home once more. How wonderful is Gods goodness how kind he is to watch over us day and nigh and our dear ones scattered arround the world, yet they never get out of his sight. He keeps all. No one is forgotten. I do not know what I would do if I had no God to go to for help. I feel so helpless and he is so able to save all that come to him.

Dec 5 sabbeth

A very stormy day. We had a very happy day at home. Elwood went away in the afternoon. I had a nice time reading.

Dec 6 Monday

Very stormy day. Snowed all day. The children done the house work. Mr Reid made fires. I sewed on my dress. Was very busy fixing for Lizzie Perines wedding.

Dec 7 Tuesday

Very cold and snowy. Nice slaying [sleighing]. Went in the afternoon to freehold. Had a nice slay ride. Took tea with aunt margaret. Called on my sister-in-law Mrs Conover. Came home about sundown and Elwood took the slay and horses and went to Perines vill [Perrineville] to singing school.

---

[136] Empress cloth: a woolen fabric. To save precious fabric, women often remade dresses or reused fabric from older dresses. Sarah was taking apart a dress and refashioning the skirt.

[137] This marked William Reid's return home for the rest of the winter until the following April.

Dec 8 Wednesday

Very busy all day. Baked in the morning and ironed in the afternoon. Lewis
Perine and Kate came to borrow some looking glasses and lamps for the wedding.
Splendid day.

Dec 9 Thursday

Very pleasant and nice. Lewis came before breackfast for cream for ice cream
for the wedding. Tillie and Con came about sundown and staid all night. I set
my large rose geraneum out on the portico and it was like a summer day so I left
it out and forgot it until about sundown when I brought it in frozen every leaf
except two branches. Took of two or three roses & some pink verbenas and
made a nice boquet for Lizzie Perine. They had it on the mantle piece in the
parlor. It looked very nice. We had a splendid time at the wedding. The house
was full of the best and grandest of the county a very dressy company and none
looked nicer or was nicer than Kate Perine and her company Will Curby. Had a
splendid entertainment. Every thing was so nice, and Lizzie looked beautiful.[138]
We came home in Henry William Parkers slay in company with him and wife.

Dec 10 friday

Nice morning. Tillie was sick and could not go home. Had a hot fever all day.
I had my hands full with her and three of her little ones. I was up until two
oclock the night before and did not feel very smart. Slept in the room with her
and little Willie cried most of the night.

Dec 11 Saturday

Nice day. Very busy. I swept the chamber. Baked mince pies bread and cake
and killed a hod [hog]. I rit[139] the intestines. Elmira had such a head ache, I was
very tired. Went to mr Prestons in the evening after Tillies little Joe with Mr
Reid.

Dec 12 Sabbeth

Rainy morning. Went to church with my husband. Had a nice ride. Herd a
nice good sermon on charity preached by mr Cob. Con came and took his wife
and four little ones home. I straightened up the house and made beds. Lizzie
would not sweep part of the kitchen for me and I was so tired I could not sleep
and my lungs and heart hurt me so much.

---

[138] Lizzie and James J. Taylor were married at home by the Rev. D. S. Parmelee. A letter dated December
18, 1869, found at the back of Sarah's diary, also refers to the wedding. See last item in the diary.

[139] Rit: a Scottish or northern English verb meaning to slit. Sarah was probably preparing the hog intestines for sausage casings.

Dec 13 Monday

Home with my little children. Done hous work and cut Lizzies & Flora dresses. Hannah Gravat came and I cut her a Cloak. Spent a very pleasant day.

Dec 14 Tuesday

Nice day. Sewed on Lizzies dress and done house work. All well and God so good and merciful. Oh help me my Father to serve thee.

Dec 15 wednesday

Nice day. Mite warm. Done house work and sewed on Lizzies dress. In the evening read in the observer. Spent a very pleasant day.

Dec 16 Thursday

A dull morning. Came on to rain a bout eight oclock. It rained until after dinner and then it cleared off splendid. The afternoon was like a summers day and a splendid moonlight night likewise. What a beautiful earth our Heavenly Father has made for us to dwell in, and we so incensible to his goodness.

Dec 17 friday

A cool pleasant morning. Arose very early. Got breakfast over and all started for uncle Gilberts. Mr Reid Elwood and Lizzie started about sunrise & Flora and myself started soon after in the buggy. Had a very nice ride. Called at Henry Jewell. Had a nice visit. Arived home a little after dark. Found all safe.

Dec 18 Saturday

Arose early. Had a bad head ache. Baked and done house work. Worked hard all day. My little girls helped me. Gave up work in the evening and they finished up the work. I had a bad head ache all night. The moon arose early and was splendid. We enjoyed its silver loveliness very much my little girls and me.

Dec 19 Sabbeth

A nice rain in the night. Elwood went to church and not want any one with him. Lizzie wanted to go but he did not want her. We had a lovely time at home. My head aches so much I could not read much.

Dec 20 Monday

Nice day. Elmira came in the morning. Killed poltry all day. John Reid called and sent with me for the observer.

Dec 21 Tuesday

Snowed a little. Elmira washed. I helped with the house work and commenced Floras dress. Worked hard all day. Mended in the evening. Had a soar throat. Read some in the mount of olives[140] about the saviour for Flora.

Dec 22 wednesday

A very stormy day. Elmira cleaned the citchen floor. I had a bad head ache and could not sew and so I cleaned a pantry. My little girls helped me. Sewed some in the evening.

Dec 23 Thursday

A nice day. I sewed on Flora dress mended pants for Elwood. Just at night I went up stairs made beds, swept the chamber, came down, cleaned brasses, and scowered tins and mixed doughnuts. Read some in the New Y observer. Read in the bible had prayers. Went to bed had a sweet sleep. Elmira went home about dusk. I commenced the chamber about sun down. Went to bed at nine oclock.

Dec 24 friday

The most eleghant day for the time of year any one ever saw. It was like a summers day. I was very busy. Got breckfast. Mixed potato bread six or seven loaves made four mince pies and four squash pies and baked doughnuts. Elmira came about ten oclock in the mourning and dampened clothes and ironed some. I mended clothes in the evening.

Dec 25 Saturday 1869

A dull warm morning. Fixed early and went to Tillies to eat rost turkey. Had a splendid time. Very nice dinner. All well. Aunt susan was there and uncle Gilbert. Got home about dusk. Had a nice ride. Met Ely Reid and Johny and all the rest been to see Feeby[141] and took dinner with her.

Dec 26 Sabbeth

Very dull and rainy. Did not go to church. Spent a very pleasant day. I read in the obser [New York Observer] and bible. All well and God so good.

Dec 27 Monday

A rainy day. Elmira washed and I looked over her time that she has made.[142] She has been home so much and I have had the work to do. Not very well some time.

---

[140] Rev. James Hamilton, D.D., *The Mount of Olives; and Other Lectures on Prayer* (New York: R. Carter, 1846). Hamilton (1814-1867) was a prolific writer on religious topics; *The Mount of Olives* went through several editions between 1846 and 1875.

[141] Phebe Reid: a cousin, the daughter of William Reid's eldest brother, James.

[142] In the front of Sarah's diary is a page listing hours worked and tasks performed by Elmira.

Dec 28 Tuesday

A stormy day. I finish looking over my dira [diary] to see how many days Elmira has been here and mended some and sewed on Flora flounce. In the evening Mr Nelson Rue came and staid all night. We enjoyed his company very much.

Dec 29 wednesday

A dull day but did not rain. Elmira renched up the clothes and I done house work, and went to freehold in the after noon and bought me a rag carpet for the citchen and took Elmira to the cars to go to Henrys Jewells and I am affraid she has got a bad cold. She was so chilly on the road. She went over to her home and the walk make her so warm she was in such a hurry. Mr Reid has just come home from the corner.[141]

Dec 30 thursday

Nice day. Very busy baking bread mince pies cake and dough nuts, and fixing for company in the evening. My little girls was all the help I had to help me, and I had to ask them so much. They stand so much it worries me very much. It was a very warm pleasant day.

Dec 31 friday

Very warm beautiful day. Very busy. Churned dressed chickens and turkey. Lizzie cleaned the kitchen floor. I cleaned windows stewed cramberries and done house work. The day was like a summers day. Elmira Gravat & Matilda Patterson called a few minutes. I am very tired to night. I have been on my feet all day. It is the last day of the year. I have had a very busy year but God has been so good to me and mine. I ought to prais him all the time for he has been so merciful to us as a family.

> Oh for a heart to prais to prais my God
> A heart from sin set free
> A heart that always feels thy blood
> So freely shed for me
> goodness and mercy has followed me
> All the days of my life. and I will
> dwell in the house of the Lord forever.

[141] Probably Mount's Corner [West Freehold].

Jan 1 Saturday 1870

The new year commenced very beautiful and warm. I was up early and fixed for company, but I was disapointed. Mrs Sherreff Conover did not come. Mrs Preston came with Con and Tillie and their two little girls. We had eleven to take dinner and we enjoyed their company very much. They went away about four oclock and we fixed and went to uncle Johny Jewells and spent the evening. Had a splendid time. Annie Jewell and Freeman was home.[144] We came home about eleven oclock.

Jan 2 Sabbeth

A very stormy day. Could not go to church and it was communion. I was sorry. It is the second sabbeth it has rained. I had a nice time reading in the mishionary herald[145] and in the bible.

Jan 3 Mondy

A splendid day. Very busy fixing for company and had company to dinner my nephew Johny Reid and two calls mr Charles Gravat and Elmira. I was on my feet all day was very tired at night. Made currullers in the evening. Johny Reid wanted to trade a brown horse for jenny. I am affraid I will have to give jenny up yet and I shall be so grieved to do so. Mr Reid gave her me when she was a colt. He said I always kept any thing I had, and he gave her to me to keep, and then Elwood and Mr Reid has wanted me to part with her so many times and I would not. She is so gentle and nice and such a good strong horse always works with a work horse and drives with a fast horse to the carriage and I can drive her any where. She never gets frightened.

Jan 4 Tuesday

A very splendid day. Arose early. Expected company to spend the day. They came about eleven oclock in the morning. We had a very nice time. Uncle Johny Jewell and aunt Haried and cousin Charly Jewell and Kate and Freeman Jewell and Annie and Charly four little children and Ritchard Reid with my own family. A good table full and we had a splendid time all so pleasant. I done the work with the children and Annie help me some set the dinner table. I am very tired to night but I am going to hem some table napkins. The sun arose very Eleghant.

---

[144] Ann Amelia (Jewell) and Freeman Jewell, her husband. Annie was Sarah's cousin, the daughter of John and Harriet Jewell.

[145] *The Missionary Herald* was a monthly publication of the American Board of Foreign Missions. Besides the proceedings of the Board it ran articles on foreign countries, reports and letters from missionaries, reports on women's work for missions, and maps and interesting engravings of exotic places.

Jan 5 Wednesday

Very nice day. Flora and me done the work. Very busy all day. In the afternoon I altered Flora a dress finished it in the evening. Lizzie went to school the first day since Christmas.

Jan 6 Thursday

Nice cool morning. Lizzie and Flora went to school. Mr Reid and me went to Mr William Davisons to see Sam to get him to take the observer. I have a club of six signers for it and he is one.[146] We had a splendid visit. They have a very nice house very roomy and new. We came home in the evening. It rained mite hard. We had Edigah Reid[147] and Cab Reid to stay all night. Mended stockings in the evening.

Jan 7 friday

A beautiful cold morning bright sunshiny day. All alone most of the day. Done the house work. I ironed the ironing for the week and washed Elwood a fine shirt and made me almost an apron and mended two shirts and under cloths for the children. The children staid all night at Mrs Gravats, without permission.

Jan 8 Saturday

Nice day. I was very busy. A very cold day. I baked and made doughnuts pies and cake and bread. The children help me some. In the afternoon Tillie Applegate and her brother and Miss Jackson and another young lady they spent the evening. Went away about one oclock.

Jan 9 Sabbeth

A very cold day and the roads so rough the horses could not go off of a walk and we have to go near six or seven miles to the old tennet church. I had a lovely time. Read my Dr Elexanders religious experiance. [Alexander's *Thoughts on Religious Experience*] John Reid and Ely[148] took dinner with us. Johny staid all night.

---

[146] In 1870, the *New York Observer* initiated a subscription incentive program in which subscribers who brought in new subscribers got reduced rates. A person bringing in 18 new subscribers received a $55 Grover & Baker Sewing Machine. (*New York Observer*, December 30, 1869)

[147] Edigah Reid: possibly Elijah Reid, the 21-year-old son of Elijah Reid, a prosperous farmer in Manalapan.

[148] John and Ely Reid: the sons of James and Mary (Ely) Reid, William Reid's eldest brother.

Jan 10 Monday

Cold day. Mr Reid went to the marl pits.[149] Elwood went home with Johny. I done the house work all alone. Edith Anderson[150] came in the afternoon. Elwood came in the evening.

Jan 11 Tuesday

Splendid day like a summers day. Mr Reid went to squancum[151] for marl. Elwood went for a wash woman. She came and washed. Aunt margaret and uncle Benny came and took dinner. Uncle Johny Jewell called. Leander Jewell came in the afternoon and staid all night. I was so glad to see him. He has been so sick with the typhoid fever.

Jan 12 Wednesday

A very splendid day. I baked some pies and cake and done the rest of the house work and was so tired set down after three oclock coverd my head and read some in Md Demesess fashion book [*Demorest's Illustrated Monthly*]. Leander Jewell came about four oclock and staid all night. We had a very nice time with him. We enjoy his company very much. Mr Reid churned for me in the evening. I was very tired and Lizzie did not want to make her own bed.

Jan 13 thursday

Nice warm day warm as may. Leander went home in the afternoon. We was sorry to part with him. He has been so long coming to pay us a visit. I done the house work and cooking and ironed in the fournoon. In the afternoon I mended the childrens dresses and finished me an apron. Elwood was sick with a cold. I was very much frightened about him. I was affraid he was going to have the scarlot fever. Dull cloudy night.

---

[149] William Reid was going to marl pits in the nearby area. Rights of way were established in some areas to allow farmers access local pits. Whether Reid was digging marl himself, or purchasing it already dug isn't clear. The fertilizing of fields with marl, a soil of clay and calcium carbonate from ancient deposits of marine life, was a traditional English farming technique. In New Jersey a stratum of marl, several miles wide and relatively near the surface, stretches from the Atlantic Coast below Sandy Hook to the lower Delaware. The discovery of significant "greensand" marl deposits in the 1820s began a thriving commerce in marl and a dramatic renewal of agricultural production in the area. Horace Greeley wrote "...half the entire region [the New Jersey Pine Barrens] is underlaid by at least one stratum of the famous marl...which has already played so important and beneficent a part in the renovation and fertilization of large districts in Monmouth, Burlington, Salem and other counties." [Greeley, *What I Know of Farming*, 1871, p. 166]

[150] Edith Anderson: a servant in the home of Sarah's aunt and uncle, Margaret and Benjamin Van Cleve.

[151] Squankum, about 5 miles northwest of Manasquan, outside what is now Allaire State Park, was the site of extensive commercially developed marl pits and a terminus of the Freehold & Squankum Railroad.

Jan 14 friday

Real cold morning. Elwood is better. Was up all day cutting vitlings [whit-tlings] around the citchen fixing an apperatus to churn with. I done the house work and ironed in the afternoon. Worked hard all day very tired at night. Mended some in the evening. Uncle Benny was here all day helping men thrash outs [oats]. Commenced to snow about three oclock or half after. Snowed and stormed all the evening. I have been thinking of those who are half clothed and fed this cold wether.

Jan 15 Saturday

A stormy day. Day was very busy baking. My two little girls helped me. I sewed some in the afternoon and mended shirts and stockings in the evening. My eyes hurt me very much when I was done.

Jan 16 Sabbeth

A nice day. All went to church but Elwood. He kept house and dinner near ready beef stake on the stove cooking. In the afternoon Lizzie and Flora went to see how aunt Harriet was and did not come back until their Father went for them after dark. I was all alone while he was gone and had a sweet time thinking of Gods goodness and tender mercies.

Jan 17 Monday

Rainy morning. The children went to school. In the afternoon Mr Reid took us and went after the children to school and made aunt margaret a visit. Had a nice time. Came home in the evening.

Jan 18 Tuesday

Splendid day. Arose early. The children helped me clear away the breckfast table and I took them to school with jenny Lynn and the buggy. Called as I came back on Mrs Henry Wm Parker[152] and the Widow Parker Mrs Shepherd Mrs Storm and Mrs Crawford[153] to see if they would sign for the Observer and drove to uncle Johny's for oat bags. Mr Reid wanted to take away oats. Came home got dinner. Sewed on Floras worsted dress in the afternoon. Knit in the evening.

Jan 18 [19] Wednesday

Nice warm day beautiful. I washed some and done house work. Had a very

---

[152] Mary Elizabeth (Reid) Parker: a cousin of Sarah's and William's married to Henry William Parker. Some of Sarah and William's farmland abutted the Parkers.

[153] All neighbors on the main road to Freehold.

bad head ache. Cooked and worked all day. There was prayer meeting in the evening. The children went with Mr Gravats girls. Elwood and Mr Reid rubbed my head until it was almost well.

Jan 19 [20] Thursday

Splendid day. I ironed and done house work all the forenoon. In the afternoon went with Mr Reid to Tillies. Had a bad head ache all day. Arived there safe. Found them all well. Staid all night. About nine oclock the pain left my head.

Jan 20 [21] friday

Nice morning. Started for home. Got home about eleven oclock found all safe. The children gone to school. Got dinner cleared it off and aunt Mary Reid my sisterinlaw and Johny came and staid all night. Was glad to see her. I was very busy. Made buiscuite for tea and cooked chickens. Cleared it away and mixed doughnuts and made two kinds of sponge for potato bread. Mr Reid churned for me and I took up the butter. Had prayers and went to bed at ten oclock very tired.

Jan 21 [22] Saturday

Nice morning. Very busy baking. The children helped do the house work and to get dinner. After dinner Mary and Johny went home. I was sorry to have them go I had so little leisure while they was here to enjoy their company. We have a very nice colt sick. We all think so much of for it is so gentle. We have petted it very much. They gave it some medason [medicine] about one oclock and it appeared better but about nine oclock at night it died.

I was sick when Lizzie came in and told me she saw it die. She cried about it. It was her colt. It was worth seventy five dollars. I felt very bad about it. It was more than we was able to lose, but I was thankful that God had touched us so lightly. If it had been a dear one it would have been dreadful.

Lizzie baked my doughnuts and we went to bed. Elwood went to see Garret Conover and staid all night.

Jan 22 [23] Sabbeth

Rained a little in the morning and cleared off to late for us to fix to go to church. We had a very nice time at home. I had a nice time reading & the children is reading the bible through. Mrs Shepherd came over in the afternoon and Elmira took dinner with us.

Jan 23 [24] Monday

A very dull day. I was very busy blacking stoves.[154] Blacked three and Lizzie

---

[154] Cast iron stoves had to be blacked with stove black, a waxy material, to keep them from rusting. A rusty stove would eventually wear thin and crack.

cleaned the citchen floor and swept the chamber, and in the afternoon we finished two dresses and mended some. Uncle Johny Jewell took tea with us. Mr
Reid went home with him to plaster a little wall.

> our children
> Saviour, these to thee we bring,
> To be sheltered 'neath they wing;
> By the love that brougt thee down
> From thy kingdom and thy crown
> By the tender ties now given
> Precious souls to link to heaven,
> Draw our children, Lord to thee,
> Ere the darker days they see!
>
> Gently lead them in the way
> Ending in Thy perfect day,
> Teach their infant lips the song
> Sung thy angel choirs among;
> Then, within thy holy keeping,
> Saved from sin, from saddest weeping,
> These our loved ones blest must be,
> Blest forever, Lord, with Thee.[155]

Jan 24 [25] Tuesday

Stormed in the night and rained very hard until nearly nine oclock in the
morning. The children wanted to go to school so much that they walked to
school. The ground was running like a brook but I could not prevail on their
Father or Elwood to take them to school. Done housework and mended Elwoods
overcoat and some shirts.

Jan 25 [26] wednesday

Very nice morning. All went to see aunt Mary and Johny. Had a very muddy
ride and a nice visit. Took dinner with them. Ely wife was sick. I was sorry to do
so little for her and Mr Reid kept at me to let Johny have my horse that I
thought so much of. It was painful to be so near of traiding Jenny away. She is so
gentle and nice. Such a beautiful silky coat and a light cream coulored main in
such a wavy fleece that it looked like fethers moving in the breze. It is the most
splendid main any horse ever had, and then I loved her so much. It was joy to
me to see her travel. I started for home with a heavy heart to think I must
always give up my wish to gratify my husband and family. I was always the one to

---

[155] Sarah occasionally entered poetry in her diary, verses that were taken from the magazines and newspapers she read. I have not been able to identify the source of this poem.

give up my way to pleas some one and no one pleased at last, but I am deeply grieved about it. We had a bad dark ride through mud up to the hub in places. We called to see Mrs Peter Clayton[156] and spent part of the evening very pleasantly. She has a lovely babe of eleven months. The children and Elwood went to singing school. We came home about twelve oclock.

Jan 26 [27] thursday

A very lovely day. The woman came to wash. Was very busy doing house work and made a jelly cake in the afternoon. It was nice. We are all well. Such a kind heavenly keeper. We ought always rejoice that Jesus always lives. The knolledge of him is anough to fill all earth with the most joyous rapture. Wondrous goodnes the friend of sinners, yes tis He with garments dyed on calverey.

Jan 27 Friday

A most lovely day that ever any won saw in January. I was home all alon all day and worked very hard. Done house work and dressed chickens. In the afternoon Ironed until dark. Got tea and mended clothes in the evening. I went to bed so tired my arm ached all the night and I had to go to bed and say my prayers without reading any. My feelings was so hurt that I could not have a minute to read my bible. I was so full I could scarcely say my prayers for crying. I had worked hard all day and I would have been so glad to have a little time to read. Mr Reid and Elwood went to cort to hear Hendricksons Trial.[157] I took my dinner alone and was so impressed with the view of Gods great goodness to me that I shed tears of gladnes and gratitude.

Jan 28 Saturday

A very stormy day. I was sick worked sick. My arms was so weak I could do but little. Flora staid home from school and done the house work. Lizzie went to school and Charly Jewell brought her home from school.

Jan 30 Sabbeth

A very nice day. Mr Reid and Lizzie and Flora went with him to church. Elwood and me staid home. I was smarter. I read some to the children.

Jan 31 Monday

Nice day. Lizzie staid home from school and cleaned the citchen and I baked.

---

[156] Mrs. Peter Clayton: Mary E. (Reid) Clayton, William Reid's younger sister.

[157] This trial stemmed from the assault on Wilson Hendrickson by Esek and James Hartshorne on October 22, 1869 that Sarah mentions in her diary on October 24, 1869. The Hartshornes were found guilty on January 31 and fined $200. [Monmouth Democrat, February 3, 1870]

About ten oclock Fannie Conover came. She is a niece of mine a very sweet girl. We was very glad to see her.

I was very busy all day two. Miss Conover came in the afternoon and took tea with me.

Feb 1 Tuesday

Nice day. Lizzie went to school and Flora staid home and helped me dress chickens and do house work. I swept the chamber and washed windows. I was so tired I was almost sick.

Feb 2 Wednesday

A cool morning. We had the pleasure of the company of Elijah Reid and wife and little daughter.[158] We had a nice time. We was glad to see them. Tillie and Con came and took dinner with us, they went away early, for they left the children home.

Feb 3 Thursday

A nice cool day. I went to feehold in the afternoon and bought Lizzie a school shall [shawl], and Mr Reid traded Jenny away to Ely Reid. He had went on Tuesday and fetched her home from Johnies. His was two fast for our horse, and I was so glad I said she should not go away again but on Thursday afternoon Ely came and he would trade although I was so opposed to it and was so sorry to part with her. I had a good cry to aunt Margarets and went on to freehold with my red eyes and my heart almost broke. I could see the ugly white face and one white eye and one dark one every time I awoke and with a sad heart remembered Jenny was gone.

Feb 4 friday

Nice day. Done house work in the morning and folded clothes in the afternoon. Ironed and prepared tea and mended clothes until bed time and was so tired I could not sleep. My arms ached all night and in the morning I was sick and weak. I could not work. Flora staid home and done the house work. I done nothing but read a little.

Feb 6 sabbeth

A nice cool morning. Mr Reid and his two little daughters went to church . Elwood staid home with me and helped to get dinner.

---

[158] Elijah Reid, a prosperous farmer in Manalapan, his wife Phebe and six-year old daughter, Margaret.

Feb 7 Monday

A splendid cool day. I went with Mr Reid to the funeral of Mrs Sarah Parker.[159] She was a very old lady and a woman who went to church and night Meeting as long as she could. I liked her very much. She was beautiful in death. She looked as if asleep so natural and so seet [sweet] with the choicest flowers. After the funeral we went to see Sherreff Conover and took dinner with him and family. Mary Laird and John her husband was there.[160] We called to settle with Mr Chambers at the Instatute for Elwoods schooling.[161]

Feb 8 Tuesday

A very stormy day. Snowed in the morning and turned to rain in the afternoon . We had a very happy day. All home to enjoy ourselves as we loved best. I sewed some in the afternoon on the trimmings of flora dress.

Feb 9 Wednesday

A very blowing morning. Every thing beautiful bright with Gods splendid snow so pure and eleghant. I always feel as if I almost envied the ground such a beautiful spotless covering of purity. I was very busy baking bread mince pies and cake. Flora staid home from school to help me. Mr Reid and Elwood went to perines will [Perrineville] to oxen drw [draw?].[162]

Feb 10 Thursday

A nice cool day with some snow scawls [squalls] through the day. We went with Mr Reid to Englishtown. Had a splendid slay ride. Took dinner with Mr John H Laird, his wife is a niece of Mr Reids. We had a splendid visit and such a nice dinner. Lizzie and Flora enjoy their visit very much. They have five beautiful children the eldest about ten. I engaged a wheeler & wilson sewing machine of I 'r Laird.[163]

---

[159] Sarah D. Parker: the widow of Joseph T. Parker, died in Freehold on February 6, 1870 at the age of 83.

[160] John H. Laird: a dealer in dry goods and groceries with a store at the corner of Spring and Main Streets in Englishtown.

[161] The Rev. A. G. Chambers was the principal of the Freehold Institute, established in 1844, which was located in Freehold on Institute Avenue. A boys' school, it advertised that its students "were thoroughly prepared for Colleges or business . . . "

[162] Sarah may be referring to an ox draw, a contest between farmers driving teams of oxen pulling heavy weights.

[163] Having a sewing machine of one's own was a tremendous boon to the housewife, who was still likely to make most of her family's clothing. By the 1870s there were numerous makes of machines on the market at reasonable cost. Sewing machines could be bought on time, and some companies offered trade-in allowances for old machines.

Came home by Mr Vanclef[164] and spent the evening with them. Had a very nice time. Came home about twelve oclock.

Feb 11 Friday

A nice day. I was very busy. Had a woman to wash. In the afternoon David Appelgate[165] came and staid all night. We was all very glad to see him. He is my cousin and a very nice young man.

Feb 12 Saturday

Nice day. Pretty busy cooking and doing house work. In the afternoon Elwood went home with Davy. Johny Reid took dinner with us. I ironed in the afternoon and was very tired when night came but God is so good. I am not thankful enough for his care which is so wonderful to us. If I had a thousand tongs to sing his prais eternily would be too short to tell the smallest part of his goodness.

Feb 13 Sabbeth

Went to the old church. Herd Mr Cob preach a very good sermon. Came home and spent the rest of the day reading. The west was an eleghant sight so gorgeous and lovely was setting sun.

Feb 14 Monday

A nice day. Lizzie was almost sick with a cold and Flora was not much better. Con and Tillie took dinner with us and went home early. We was very glad to see them. It rained in the evening and has the appearence of a stormy night. I have felt very sadly part of the day to think my children thinks so little of eternal things. If they only love the dear saviour I would feel they was safe for this world and for eternity. I have always expected them to love the saviour while young. I have prayed with and for them dayly and with tears led them to the saviours feet. My only son is twenty one and no hope of heaven. I am so grieved that he does not love the saviour.

Feb 15 Tuesday

A very eleghant morning just as nice as may. In the afternoon it clouded up and began to rain and continued ail the evening. I was doing house work nearly all day. I ironed part of the day.

Feb 16 Wednesday

A splendid day like a summers day. I spent the forenoon doing house work. In

---

[164] Probably Thompson Van Cleaf: whose home was on the road from Englishtown to Blacks Mills, a likely route for Sarah to have taken home.
[165] David Applegate: the son of Gilbert and Susan (Reid) Applegate.

the afternoon I went to see Mrs Applegate. She has been sick two or three weeks. Had a nice ride in the evening. Took a splendid ride with Mr Reid to Mounts corner [West Freehold] with rough and ready. She did trot splendid. I wanted to stop and see aunt Margaret but he did not wish to stop and I was so sorry to come by.

Feb 17 Thursday

Nice day. Very busy baking bread mince pies apple pies and made doughnuts. I was very tired when I was done. In the after noon I read some in Md Demoress book [*Demorest's Illustrated Monthly*]. Was very much disapointed about going to prayer meeting. It commenced to sprinkle about time to go but did not rain much.

Feb 18 friday

A very stormy day. Mr Reid and Flora went to see Tillie in the storm and staid all night. The storm was in their backs a going and they could not come home so well on account of the rain in their faces coming home. Elwood and Lizzie and myself spent the day very happily. In the evening we eate hickery nuts dough nuts, and had a nice time. In the forenoon I mended Mr Reid's pants. In the afternoon I made Elwood some neckties.

Feb 19 Saturday

A nice day. I swept the chamber in the morning. In the afternoon cleaned the citchen floor and mended clothes. If I could only see my dear children loving the dear saviour and trying to serve him I should be so glad. I have always thought they would early seek the saviours love first.

Feb 20 Sabbeth

Went to church with Mr Reid and our two little girls. Herd a very good sermon on good morals from Mr Cob. It was a splendid day. Saw some friends. Rained in the afternoon.

Feb 21 mondays 1870

Very cold morning. Great change in the night cold all day. Elwood was stormstaid[166] all night. Rained almost all night and came home about ten in the morning. The children done the most of the house work and I commenced Elwoods some shirts. Very cold night. I am affraid some one will freeze to death to night. What a mercy we are all home safe and well. We have such a good kind God we have to always watch over us and guard us safe from every harm.

---

[166] Stormstaid: a Scottish colloquialism meaning to be detained by the weather.

Feb 22 tuesday

A very rough cold day. Elwood carted two loads of marl from the corner and seemed very cold when he came home. In the afternoon Mr Reid went and got one load. I spent most of the day sewing on Elwoods shirts. Mended stockings in the Evening.

Feb 23 wednesday

Nice pleasant day. Got warmer in the night. We was invited to Mr John Reids a cousin of ours. We had a nice visit and came home about dusk. Had a call in the evening Mr John Applegate and my nephew Johny Reid. After singing school Elwood brought Carrie Reid home with him and she staid all night and we had the pleasure of her company all day.

Feb 24 thursday

A very nice day. Pretty cool. The woman washed for me and I done house work and sewed on Elwoods shirts. Had a very pleasant time with Carrie Reid and Johny Reid. Had them to dinner. Towards evening the weather grew coulder. Very cold at night. Carrie and Elwood went to singing school. Mr Reid and my little girls are home with me. So many comforts and God so good and kind to us.

My two little girls has been trying to play dominose with pieces of paper and I have tried to persuade them that every idle minute is lost and will have to give account to God for their lost time.

Feb 25 Friday

Nice day. I was ironing nearly all day. Carrie Reid was here until afternoon and Elwood took her home. The children done the most of the house work. I was so tired at night I was almost sick.

Feb 26 Saturday

A nice day. I made pies and done house work. Black Mag and bennie[167] came here and wanted so many things it took me some time to get her supplied. I gave them their dinner and what they could carry home. Her husband was sick. Sewed some in the afternoon on Elwoods clothes.

Feb 27 Sabbeth

A nice cool morning. Was part ready for church when Mr Reid began to hurry me as he always does. When I said I would stay home but Flora and Lizzie

---

[167] Both Freehold and Manalapan had black communities at the time. The U.S. Census of 1870 enumerated 310 black residents of a population of 4233 in Freehold and a black population of 193 of a population of 2387 in Manalapan.

was so disapointed I concluded to go and Mr Reid said we should not go. I felt
very much provoked but said nothing. It is too bad for men to controll their
wives in every thing and they are so nice before marriage. No one thinks they
are always to give up their wishes to pleas those that are no better than they are.
I have always been so fond of pease I would bear any thing for pease, but any
one must keep on bearing.

If I can only have a home where Jesus is I shall be willing to bear all of earths
troubles, but they will chafe some times. It stormed in the afternoon and snowed
towards morning. The ground was covered.

Feb 28 Monday

A very pleasant morning but stormed in the afternoon. I was about Elwoods
going away to Clark Perines to be a clerk in his store.[168] We are so sorry to have
him go but he thinks it will be better than farming but I am so much affraid he
may learn bad ways, or ingure his health. His path has been so smoothe at home.
Every wish I have tried to gratify and make home so pleasant for him. His days
has passed without frowns or cross words from me and with a scarce a reproving
look from me. He was always a good pleasant boy never needed a cross word. If
he was only a christtain and loved the dear saviour I should be so happy but he
is in [?] a very kind and merciful God.

Tuesday March 1 1870

A dull unpleasant day. Elwood went to Clark Perines to tend store. Mr Reid
took the children and me with him to aunt Margarets and spent the day.

wednesday March 2

Very busy baking, and sewed some in the afternoon. Felt worried about
Elwoods going away.

March 3 Thursday

Nice cool day. Very busy finishing Elwood shirts. All well and God is good.

March 4 friday

Nice day. Washed a little in the morning and ironed some. Very tired at
night.

March 5 saturday

Nice cool day. Done house work and went to feehold in the afternoon and

---

[168] D. C. Perrine: a merchant with a dry goods store in Freehold on Main Street. Perrine advertised that
his was the "cheapest store in town." It carried carpets, crockery, wagon wares, boots and shoes, win-
dow shades, ready-made clothing, building hardware, white lead and zinc, flagstones, nails, lime,
cement, coal, and sewing machines, among other wares. [*Monmouth Democrat*, July 29, 1869]

wated. Elwood was out of the store and call at my sisterinlaw Mrs Samuel Conovers[169] and had a nice chat.

March 6 sabbeth

Nice morning. Went to hear Mr Cob preach. Had a good sermon. Stormed in the afternoon. Read for the children in the afternoon.

March 7 Monday

A very stormy morning. Elwood came home early, and towards noon Mr Reid took him in the slay to Clark Perines. It snowed all day. We went to uncle Johnies in the afternoon and had a nice visit. Came home early in the evening.

March 8 Tuesday

A very stormy morning. We was almost ready to go to Englishtown with Mr Reid to take a nice slay ride but it kept on snowing all the morning. In the afternoon we took a slay ride to call on Mrs Clayton and Elmira Gravat & on Mrs Perine and spent the evening with her and had a splendid time.

The girls was all home and I do think so much of them, and we was treated so well. They are the nicest family we ever visited.

March 9 Wednesday

Nice morning but very cool. Elwood came home from Clark Perines with his toe mashed with a barrel of cement. I was frightened when I saw him. He was lame and I did not know how bad he was hurt. In the evening uncle Gill and his girls called.

March 10 Thursday

A nice morning. The children sewed carpet rags[170] for me and Elwood cut some and I cut in the afternoon and baked bread and pies and cake in the morning.

March 11 friday

A splendid day. Mrs Mack[171] washed for me, and Tillie and Con and their two little girls took dinner with us and wanted us to put out our place to them to farm but I am not so fond of moving. I was almost sick with a cold.

---

[169] Mrs. Samuel Conover: Matilda (Reid) Conover

[170] The girls were sewing strips of cloth end to end for use in weaving or braiding rag rugs. B. Schlosser, a Freehold carpet weaver, advertised in the *Monmouth Democrat* that he would weave carpets at short notice with either wool, cotton, or linen warps.

[171] Mrs. Mack: hired household help, probably the wife of Joseph Mack, an Irish laborer, whose home was nearby.

March 12 Saturday

Nice day. Mr Vlet called. I was ironing in the forenoon, the children done part of the house work. Very dull in the afternoon. Stormed before dark and all night stormed and blowed dredfully all night. I was so thankful that our little family was all home safe, except Tillie and she has a home of her own and a kind husband and four babes. The eldest is six years old.

March 13 Sabbeth

A very stormy morning. Was a little moderate about eleven oclock. We was all home and a very pleasant time reading and the children learned verses.

March 14 Monday

Arose early and Mr Reid went to New York. Elwood took him to the station and went away about twelve and is not home yet and it is eight oclock and the children and myself are all alone. It has been a splendid day and it is an eleghant moonlight night.

March 15 Tuesday

Nice day. Made fire and got breackfast. Elwood was very sleepy. He was up late. Before noon we saw Mr Reid coming home. He had sold his horse and came back all safe. Elwood went to freehold in the afternoon to Clark Perines and Mr Reid went to Conover Prestons. I baked and Elwood & Lizzie churned.

March 16 Wednesday

Very rainy day. Stormed and blowed all night dredfully. I was not very well all day, had a bad headache. Lizzie rubed it away almost. I took a little nap in my chair, in the afternoon mended stockings and had a nice time with my little ones.

March 17 Thursday

A very bitter cold day. The wind is most cutting, but Florence would go to school although we did not want her to go and her Father told her not to go. It was too cold and she was almost perished but she got no cold. I was not well but I cleaned the oilcloth in the sitting room in the afternoon. Swept part of the chamber and sewed some. In the evening mended stockings and fixed to bake, bread. Had another sweet good night.

March 18 Friday

A nice cool morning. Bright and beautiful. I was very busy baking bread pies and two kinds of cake and cleaning up. Lizzie was cleaning the citchen and very busy until tea time when Con came and took tea with us.

March 19 Saturday

Nice day. Had company all day, a cousin of Mr Reids. Was very much pleased with them. Mr John Reid and wife and two daughters & Miss Boughtton. Was disapointed in the evening abought seeing Elwood. Lizzie was not well.

March 20 Sabbeth

Nice day. Went to church. Herd Mr Cob Preach. Came home through Freehold. Called to see Elwood and aunt Margaret. Had a nice time reading in the afternoon in dodriges's rise and progres.[172]

March 21 Monday

A dull misty morning. Done house work and sewed on Lizzies dres. In the afternoon Mr Vancleft called and in the evening Mary Vancleft[173] & two Miss Gravats called and I was very tired when night came.

March 22 Tuesday

Splendid day. Expected company to spend the day but they did not come and the children went to see Ellie Bearmore[174] and I was all alone all the afternoon and had a very pleasant time. I love to feel alone with God. He is so good. I love to think of his goodness and shed tears of gratitude when no eye but his is on me. Mr Reid and the children cam home about sundown.

March 23 Wednesday

A beautiful clear bright morning but very windy. We had the company of Davison Reid and wife and two daughter and likewise Elijahs Reid two daughters. They came about ten oclock and we had a nice time. I enjoyed their visit very much. In the afternoon Lizzie had company in the afternoon the two Miss Gravats & Miss VanCleft and Miss Bearmore and Miss Frances. We had fifteen to take tea.

March 24 Thursday

A very blustery blowey day. The children went to school and I was all alone until four oclock. Had a lovely time. The first thing after they was gone I washed the dishes and saw a lovely flower just bursting out. It was so fresh and lovely I shed tears when I saw it. Oh I thought God is so good to Mortals and I so incen-

[172] Philip Doddridge, D.D., *The Rise and Progress of Religion in the Soul illustrated in a course of serious and practical addresses suited to persons of every character and circumstance*. First published in 1744 in Philadelphia, this volume by Doddridge (1702-1751) became a classic guide to Calvinist piety and went through countless editions. Sarah may have been familiar with the 1843 edition published by the Presbyterian Board of Publication.

[173] Perhaps a member of the Thompson Van Cleaf family.

[174] Elinor Bearmore: the nine-year-old daughter of neighbors.

cible to his goodness. Then I swept the parlor & sitting room & kitchen and then cleaned thirty eight knives and forks besides spoons then took dinner all alone at half past twelve on bread and butter and chicken and a good cup of tea. At half past two set down to comb my head and then sewed in the afternoon. My oleander, it has bloomed all winter on the citchen table.

Heaven

If the promice that I in that temple should shine
    Whose light is the halo of glory divine,
    Where promised till ages on ages untold
Away to the depths of past ages had rolled
And still to the promise a limit were given,
Though ever so distant, it would not be heaven

No! Thought's piercing wings yet beyond it would fly,
In search for what yet in the distance might lie;
The glory of Heaven, through fear, would be dim,
And sadness blend still with its rapturous hymn
    Tis endless duration, unceasing delight,
That makes the blest hope of the Christian so bright
'Tis the richest of gems in his heavenly crown
That the sun of his blessedness will not go down
    With that song everlasting no fear shall be blended,
For then shall the day's of his mourning be ended;
And once in that temple, beside the pure river
The sainted no more shall be absent forever.[175]

March 25 friday

Nice morning. The children went to school and I was very busy. Had a great lot of work to do and a great deal more ambition than strength. Done the breckfast work and baked bread mince pies and cake prepared dinner cleared it away. Aunt Margaret took tea with me. I was very glad to see her. She has not been here in a great while and when night came on I found I was sick and set down. The work was done and I had worked myself sick. My arms and shoulders pained me and such a burning soarness between my shoulders that I slept but little. My arms had pained me for two weeks so I could not sleep at night.[176]

March 26 saturday

A dull day. I was sick. I got up and prepared breakfast but was so weak I could

---

[175] This poem appeared in the December 30, 1869 issue of the *New York Observer*.

[176] The cause of Sarah's symptoms is difficult to identify; they suggest exhaustion from her hard physical work.

scarcely use my arms. I could do no more. The children done the rest of the work.

We was very much disapointed that Elwood did not get home from Clark Perines. We set up until nearly eleven oclock waiting for him and Cab Reid to give them their tea.

March 27 Sabbeth

Mr Reid arose early. He knew it was going to storm, but thought he would drive to town for Elwood before it came on. He had the horses seen to and came in and it commenced to storm dreadfully. It had blown all night, and so he did not like to drive three miles facing the storm and we was so disapointed all day. The storm raged all day but we was all warm and happy inside but would have been more so if we had the two absent dear children with us but Tillie would go from us and Elwood felt he could do better than work on a farm, and so I always feel as if it is Gods will for he can easily fraustrate any of our plans if it is his will.

March 28 Monday

A very dull rainy day. I was able to do but little. The wash woman came and washed, and cleaned the citchen floor.

March 29 Tuesday

A windy cool day. Mr Reid took us all to see Tillie and my heart was sick to see her. She is worked until she is nothing but a frame and a very slender one at that. Her four little ones is two much for one to wait on and all the rest she has to do, and has so little rest at night. If I get a little smarter[177] I will take Fannie and Willie if she will let them come. Came home in the evening and could not sleep until nearly morning worrying about Tillie. I am affraid she will not live through the spring. I thought of every way and every thing to save her life. I can think of nothing but to get her something to strengthen her. I have taken cold going out and so am not so well to day.

March 30 wedness

Nice day cold day. Had a bad head ache all day and was almost sick. The children staid home from school to help me.

March 31 Thursday

Cool morning. Mr Reid went up to New York to sell a horse he had engaged to a man. I done some ironing but was not able to do it. Acksia Perine spent the afternoon with us. We was all so pleased to see her. The children drove to freehold to meet their father in the evening and see their brother.

---

[177] Smart: a colloquialism meaning brisk, active, in good health.

Aprail 1 friday

Nice day. Baked but was almost sick. Went to bed before the bread was out of the oven. Was very sick. The children done all they could for me.

Aprail 2 Saturday

Rained all day. I arose to breckfast but could not eat any so sick. Went to bed part of the day. It kept on raining and Mr Reid did not go for Elwood. The children and me did want to see him so much.

Aprail 3 Sabbeth

I wanted to go so much to church but was not able. It was dull and rainy. Mr Reid went after Elwood but did not go to church. We was so glad to see him and had a nice time. He wanted to go to see carry [Carrie] Reid after dinner but it was so rainy he did not go, and so we had him all alone to ourselves all night and as good friends as he had any where and it is such a blessing to have all our dear ones home with us.

Aprail 4 Monday

A rainy drisly morning. Mr Reid took Elwood to freehold about half past seven. I was not very smart. Lizzie and Florence done the work and churned in the afternoon. They was very lively all day and enjoyed themselves very much. It snowed and stormed hard all the afternoon.

Aprail 5 Tuesday

A very stormy day. The grownd five or six inches of snow and snowing on. Cleared off about noon. Mr King called. The children swept the chamber and I done the citchen work. Felt better. Mr Reid went to freehold in the afternon. I mended and sewed in the afternoon. It is six oclock and getting dark and I cannot see to follow the line.

> Jesus the visions of thy face
> Hath overwelming charms
> Scarce should I feel deaths cold embrace
> If christ be in my arms

Aprail 6 Wednesday

A rainy morning. It has rained every day since last Saturday. I have ironed some and mended dresses in the afternoon for the children. The sun set splendid. When it was cuite dark there was a splendid silvery light mingled with dark blue clouds and a rosie tinge like a border near the earth. Mr Reid went to freehold to see if his horse had come from new york after sunset and we spent the evening without him. Uncle bennie called.

Aprail 7 Thursday

Nice morning. I sewed some and done house work in the afternoon. Just as the sun set the west was more splendid than any thing I ever saw. It seemed as though the Glory of the promice rest must be shining through or the pearly gates ajar. Oh for a home in the skies! To lay my soul at Jesus, no matter how lowly.

Aprail 8 friday

A very splendid day. I was very busy baking. The children done the most of the house work, and we all went to freehold in the afternoon and saw Elwood and called on Mrs Sherreff Conover and Fannie. Had a splendid time. Bought the children dresses.

Aprail 9 saturday

Most beautiful day. Sewed some and uncle Johny Jewell called and Spafford Reid[178] & Elijah called and bought our fannie horse and in the afternoon Mr Reid and me went to freehold and bought some trimming for the dresses and Cab Reid took tea and went to freehold for Elwood. All well and God so good and merciful to us such worms of the dust. Oh for a heart to prais my God a heart from sin set free.

Aprail 10 Sabbeth

A nice morning. I wanted to go to church but had company and could not get the work done in time to get ready. Cab Reid was here and tillie and Con and their little ones, and I had a bad head ache. It was was better in the evening and I had a nice time reading and singing with Florence for Lizzie was two sleeppy to sing. The evening was a beautiful moon light. Little Fannie staid with us.

Aprail 11 Monday

It commenced to rain towards morning and rained all day. Lizzie went with Elwood to freehold and drove fannie home. Came all safe. I done housework and cut two shirts and run them up and sleeves and ripped Elwoods coat binding off and prepared dinner and cleared it away. Sewed hard all the afternoon. Mr Reid went to freehold with David Reid in the afternoon.

Aprail 12 Tuesday

Nice day. Florence staid home with me. I sewed on the childrens dresses. Sewed some on Elwoods coat. Mrs Mac washed. I went with Mr Reid to get a little wench.[179] Did not get her.

---

[178] Spafford W. Reid: William Reid's nephew.

[179] Wench: a colloquialism often used in the United States at the time, for a young woman of color.

Aprail 13 Wednesday

Had a bad head ache all day. Was sick with it at night and had worked all day with such a head ache. Fixed to bake at night.

Aprail 14 Thursday

Nice day. Had a bad head ache all day. It was hard work to keep at work but the baking must go on. Baked bread pies and cake and went to bed at four oclock very tired. Lay a little while and then read some in the observer [*New York Observer*].

Aprail 15 friday

Very warm beautiful day. Went to freehold in the morning and took Elwood his coat. Call at aunt Margarets and Mrs Crawfords. Came home time to get dinner and mended Mr Reid a coat and cut him a pair of pants and sent them to Mrs crawford to make. Henry Johnson has been here making garden to day. Put in peas and onions.

Aprail 16 Saturday

A dull cool day. I ironed in the morning, and was so tired before I was done that every thing turned dark before my eyes. I sit down a few minutes and then I went and lay down and took a nap about an hour and arose and had dinner. Lizzie swept the chamber and Florrence done the morning work and they prepared dinner. In the afternoon I mended some.

Aprail 17 Sabbeth

A very dull drisly morning. Commenced to storm in the morning about ten. I had a sweet day of rest. I was so thankful when I awoak and remembered it was Gods sweet day. I wanted to go to church but it was not fit. The children done the work and let me rest and read.

Aprail 18 Monday

A real bad stormy day. I sewed on the childrens dresses and mended some. Lizzie churned and made me a jelly cake and Florence made me a molasses cake. Had a very pleasant time. Mr Reid was home and the children home from school and little Fannie is here with us and a very sheet [sweet] child she is. We sing some every day or night some of the sabbeth school hymns.

Aprail 19 Tuesday

Mr Reid went to see Spafford Reid about a horse and went to freehold in the afternoon. Fetched Mr Joseph Clayton[180] home with to stay and take care of his horses and things.

Aprail 20 Wednesday

Mr Reid went to new york in the morning train.[181] I was very sorry to have him go. When Mr Clayton came back with the horses I went after tillie and brought her and her four little ones with me home. She has not been to stay with me for a long time. We had a nice ride. Stoped and gave Mrs Vandevere some flower roots. Called at Garrets.

Aprail 21 Thursday

Nice day. Sewed some and done house work. Set out some flower roots.

Aprail 22 friday

Nice day. Done housework and tended babies some and sewed some.

Aprail 23 Saturday

Nice day. Very busy baking and doing housework. Aby jane Gravat called.[182]

April 24 Sabbeth

Nice day. Went with Elwood to church and read some in the afternoon and took care of the babies.

April 25 Monday

A dull day. Mrs Mack was her for me, and the children went to uncle Johneys and spent the day. Tillie and me sewed on the childrens dresses. Sallie Gravat[183] called and I gave her some pink roots. Very tired at night. Set down to sew at three oclock.

April 26 Tuesday

Nice day. Aunt Margaret and uncle Benny spent the day with me and we had a good time. Tillie and her four little ones are here and we enjoyed ourselves very much. Tillie went to the corner and got a letter from Mr Reid. I have been so uneasy all day about him that it came very acceptable.

---

[180] Joseph Clayton: an older man brought in to help on the farm, perhaps a relative. He stayed until the end of June.

[181] William Reid began again his work routine in New York City. This meant he would be away from home for long lengths of time until late autumn.

[182] Abbie Jane Gravat: the youngest daughter in the neighboring Gravatt family.

[183] Sally Gravat could have been either neighbor Mrs. Sally Gravat or her 16 year old daughter.

April 27 Wensday

A beautiful day. I went in the morning to take Tillie home. Had a splendid ride. Drove black fanny and rough and ready. Call on Mrs Denice. Came home at four oclock. Found all safe. Aunt Susan staid all night. Rain in the evening.

April 28 Thursday

A nice day. Had a splendid time. Aunt Margaret aunt Harriet and aunt Susan and uncle Benny spent the day with me. Uncle Benny ploughed the orchard. Had a nice thunder shower. Con was storm staid here so we had his company all night.

April 29 friday

A dull stormy morning. Had showers all day. Aunt Susan went home in the afternoon with Charly jewell and we was all alone in the afternoon. Felt very lonesome. It is the first evening we have spent alone since Mr Reid went away.

April 30 Saturday

A cool morning. Lizzie went to uncle Gilberts to get lizzie Applegate and arived home about sundown. I worked hard all day until three oclock and then Kate Perine called. I was so glad to see her. I was worked almost sick, and Elmira Gravat called in the evening and staid until late and I was so tired I did knot know how to sit up.

May 1 Sabbeth

A nice day but I did not go to church I was so tired and Lizzie Appelgate was not fixed to go. I laid down in the afternoon and was cuite rested when I got up.

May 2 Monday

Nice day. I had some time to sew on the childrens dresses and Florance went with lizzie to freehol.

May 3 Tuesday

The wash woman came and cleaned for me and I white washed the sitting room.

May 4 wenesday

Lizzie and me papered the sitting room. Was very tired at night.

May 5 [Thursday]

Nice day went in the afternoon to freehold. Set the sitting room straight in the morning.

May 6 friday

Nice day. Baked and made pies and cake. Very tired at night. Cleaned the stove and done housework all day until night. Got tea ready and was too tired to do any more. Wrote a letter to mr Reid in the evening.

May 7 Saturday

A very dull morning. Done house work. Lizzie appelgate is here. We have a nice time with her. I sewed some in the afternoon. Lizzie Apelgate & Lizzie Reid went to freehol for Elwood and did not get home until Eleven oclock. I sit up and was very tired and sleepy.

May 8 Sabbeth

A very dull morning. Wanted to go to church. Got ready but it was so drizelly and late we gave out going and went over to see aunt Harriet. They was not very well but I hurried back and got dinner and had a nice time reading in the bible and singing hyms with flora.

May 9 Monday

A very dull rainy day. Mrs Mack washed for me. The clothes did not dry. I was very busy all day. Sewed some on the childrens flounced dresses. It is so strange that mothers have such a desire to do all they can for their children even more than they have strength and for so little thanks, but they are willing to toil on expecting nothing as a reward in this world, but a home in the kingdom of love, is all and a place at jesus feet when all is over. May we not be disapoined.

May 10 Tuesday

A very dull drisly morning. I was disapointed. I expected to take aunt Margaret to Tillies. Very busy all day doing house work and Ironing and sewing. Wanted to send to the corner for a letter but it rained too bad to send to the corner. I am too busy. I do not like to have so much to attend to and so little leasure. I should like to have more time to think of my kind Heavenly Father so wonderful good to me and mine.

May 11 Wednesday

A very rainy morning. I wanted to go to Tillies for she is looking for me, but it rain too bad for me to go, but I found enough to do. I sewed some and ironed some and done house work. Wrote some in the evening. Wrote a letter to mr Reid.

May 12 Thursday

Dull morning. Very busy. All well.

Friday 13 May 1870

Went with aunt margaret to see tillie. I had a splendid time. Came a shower in the evening.

Saturday 14 May

Very busy nice day. Sewed som on the childrens dresses. I never will flounc so much again on one dress. Lizzie Applegate and Lizzie Reid went for Elwood in the evening. Went to freehold in the afternoon. Call to see Mrs buck.[184]

Sabbeth 15 May

Splendid day. Elwood and me went to charlys. Lizzie Appelgate and Lizzie Reid went to church with Elwood.

Monday 16 May

Nice day. Lizzie Appelgate went to aunt Harriets and spent the day. I was busy doing house and sewing.

Tuesday 17 May

A dull rainy morning but did not rain but little. I took Lizzie Appelgate home. Had a nice visit. Fetched aunt susan home with me.

Wensday 18 May

Nice day. Very busy making Flora a dress and cut a vest for Elwood.

May 19 Thursday

Nice day. Went with Lizzie to Mr Smiths store.[185] Took butter. Had a splendid ride.

May 20 friday

Nice dull morning. Thunder some. I was very busy baking in the morning. Aunt margaret and uncle bennie came in the afternoon and took tea with me.

May 21 Saturday

Nice day. Worked hard in the morning. Went to freehold in the afternoon after the childrens hats and when I got home Lizzie and Florence went to the station to freehold to fetch ther father home and they got caught in a shower. He was almost sick with a cold. I was so sorry to see him not well.

---

[184] Probably Margaret Buck, a neighbor on the main road to Freehold.
[185] The store at Smithburg village owned by William H. Smith.

May 22 Sabbeth

A dull morning. I done what I could for Mr Reid. Tillie and Con and their four little ones came to see us for Mr Reid was not going to be home but one day, and Elwood was home. Had a lovely time with our dear ones all home but I was so tired out I could hardly go.

May 23 monday

Nice day. Mr Reid went to new york. He said he felt a great deal better but I am affraid he did not feel as well as he said. Mrs Mack washed.

May 24 Tuesday

Nice day. I was ironing and was not very strong and done house work.

May 25 Wednesday

Aunt Margaret and uncle bennie came and uncle bennie worked with a cow. Mr Clayton had not milked clean. He had left the milk in until it was caked very bad. Uncle bennie done me a great kindnes for I could not get the milk out to save my life it was so badly caked and aunt margaret done me a great deal of good with her pressence for I felt almost discouraged. We have so much to battle with in this world and so much to over come. It is well we have a promice of sweet rest when life is past and glory begun. Ever blessed be the swet name of jesus for his dying love to bear so much to bring sinful worms to such a glorious home in the skies.

May 26 Thursday

Nice day. Lizzie staid home from school and helped me bake. I was not able to bake but we have the bread and so I had to do it. I was very tired when I got the bread in the oven. Made one cake and it was to much. I was so tired Lizzie got the dinner for me. She wanted me to go to freehold in the afternoon with me to get her a pair of shoes. We had a nice ride and received a letter from Mr Reid saying he was better. I was so thankful for Gods wonderful goodness that I rejoiced very much that I had such a kind heavenly Father that sees all our wants and does better for us than we can ask or think.

May 27 friday 1870

A very stormy blowey day. Stormed all day. The children was home from school and helped me very much with my work. I done a large ironing and could hardly speak when I was done.

May 28 saturday

A dull stormy day. I wanted so much to go to church on the sabbeth. Very busy all day. Swept the chamber and mended clothes.

May 29 Sabbeth

Very much disapointed about going to church. It was stormy and I had no one to drive for me. I was going to send Lizzie to get little Charly Jewell[186] to drive for me. I can drive pretty well but I cannot see to the horse when I get there. Rained hard. Cab called.

May 30 Monday

Nice morning. A little dull. I took the children to school and took a letter to the office to go to mr Reid and took dinner with aunt margaret. Came home and prepared dinner for Mr Clayton and about four oclock he hitched the horse and I went to the school and took the children over to Charly Jewells to see Ann Amelia Jewell[187] and Kate Jellell[188] had a new daughter a very nice babe. Had a nice time and came home. Prepared tea and finished work and read in the bible and said my prayers as I always do. Elwood called and Howard Reid.

May 31 Tuesday

Nice cool day. Very busy doing house work and commenced Elwood a vest.

June 1 wednesday

Nice morning. Went to freehold and took aunt margaret along. Had a splendid ride. Saw Elwood.

June 2 thursday

Nice day. Very busy. All well and the same kind hand guiding all things well. I baked in the morning.

June 3 friday

A dull rainy day. The children staid home from school.

June 4 Saturday

Dull in the morning. Aunt Mag and uncle bennie came and spent the day with me. We had a nice time. Aunt margaret helped me finish Elwoods white vest, and helped me make me a black lace hat, and about twelve o'clock Mr Reid came in. We was all so glad to see him home safe, and so unexpected.

June 5 Sabbeth

Nice morning. Went with Mr Reid to the tennett church to hear Mr Cob

---

[186] Charles R. Jewell: young son of Sarah's cousin, Charlie.

[187] Ann Amelia Jewell: Sarah's cousin, Charlie Jewell's sister.

[188] Catherine (Reid) Jewell: Charlie Jewell's wife. The new daughter was Mamie.

preach. Had a very good sermon. Went to tillies and took dinner. Came home about four oclock. Had a splendid ride home.

June 6 Monday

Arose very early a little after four and Mr Reid went to new york with half past six line. Very busy all day. Mrs Macky washed for me. I worked hard all day. The children and Mr Clayton picked a crate of strawberies.

June 7 Tuesday

Nice day. Rained alittle in the morning. Ironed all day until six oclock in the evening. Agusta Dubois called and annie smock, and Cab Reid came in the evening and fetched Lidia to spend some days with me. We was very glad to see her.

June 8 wednesday

Nice day. We picked strawberies Lida and Lizzie & Florance myself and Mr Clayton. We sent it with uncle Bennie.[189] In the afternoon we picked another almost but did not send it. It was a very warm day and I was so overcome with work and the sun I was almost sick but my children is so affraid they will hurt themselves, they would hardly know it if I droped down with work. A mother can work for her children until the last breath, but they are very careful of themselves.

June 9 Thursday

A nice day. Canned strawberries in the forenoon and in the afternoon went to freehold and bought Lizzie a pair of shoes for three dollars and eighty cents. Called on Mrs Shereff Conover.

June 11 [10] Friday

A very stormy day. I was baking and was so weak with work that it was hard to keep at it. I love to work but when I am worked until I am sick I would like to rest a little. I was more exposed to the storm than I have for twenty one years.

June 12 [11] Saturday

Stormy in the morning. In the afternoon Mr Reid came home and I was so glad to see him. I knew he would help me with my work all he could.

June 13 [12] Sabbeth

A very nice day. Lizzie & Lida & Florance went to church to hear a sermon

---

[189] Strawberries were a cash crop, sent to market in New York.

to children and they was so pleased they herd a gentleman that had been to jerusalem and he told them so much they was almost crazy to hear him in the afternoon but it was so far to drive and Elwood wanted the buggy so they went to sabbeth school.

Cab took Lida a home.

June 14 [13] Monday

A nice day. A little showery. We picked a crate of strawberies in the morning and uncle Bennie took them to freehold. Sent them to new york.

June 15 [14] t[uesday]

Mr Reid went to new york in the morning. Nice day. Mrs Macky cleaned the seller for me. Lizzie & Florance went to see Lida Reid. I done all the work. Was very busy. Oh the goodness of my heavenly Father. I am overcome with grattitude and Emotion then I think of his wonderful goodness. The earth is full of lovlines. The air is perfumed with the sweet flowers. Oh so wonderfull is his mercy to the children of men. Words cannot express the addoration and grattitude I feel in sight of so much goodness and love.

June 16 [15] Wednesday

A dull day. Edith Anderson helped me pick a crate of strawberies. We worked very hard to get them ready in time for the train. The children went to school. I was very tired at night. Con and tillie came about six oclock and she was very sick. I was so sorry for her but she had to go home sick.[190] Could not stay.

June 17 [16] Thursday

A little rainy. Baked in the morning. Worked hard in the forenoon. In the afternoon the children done up the dinner work and let me rest a little. Sewed in the afternoon on the childrens cambrick dresses.[191] Sam Davisson & wife took tea with me. Had a nice time with them.

June 19 [17] friday

Had a nice rain in the night. The children done the breckfast dishes and I went in the seller to clean the floor. I paid Mrs Mack seventy five cents for doing it and the floor is worse than she commenced it. A complete mud lake.[192] I had not scrubbed long when Mrs Samuel Conover & Fannie came. I was very glad to see them. They are peticular friends of mine, and so I discontinued my work in the celler. Spent the day very pleasantly with them. They took dinner & tea with

---

[190] Tillie was in the first trimester of another pregnancy.

[191] Cambric: a finely woven cotton or linen fabric, usually white.

[192] Sarah's problem with the cellar was due to the fact that the floor of her cellar would have been hard-packed earth.

me and went home a bout five oclock. Had fourteen little turkeys hatched out and put in a coop and some little ducks.

June 19 [18] Saturday

Nice day. Finished cleaning the celler floor and was very busy. Called on Mrs Perine in the afternoon.

June 20 [19] Sabbeth

Went with little charly Jewell to church. Herd Mr Cob preach. Very tired. Was not able to get ready for church but felt better on the road. Had a splendid ride.

June 22 [21] Monday [Tuesday]

Mrs Macky washed. Very busy all day perserving strawberries. Dr Tompson & Mrs Conover called in the afternoon & Lizzie Clayton toward evening.

June 21 [20] Monday

Showery in the evening. Mrs Mack washed. In the evening a little after sundown the children and myself took the horse and buggy and went to Charly Jewells and wated for charly to come home a while. He came and when I started to come home it was dark as it could be except when a brilliant flash of lightning lit up the black darkness. It was ten oclock & they wanted me to put up for the night but I had left Mr Clayton and old man waiting to put up my horse and all alone. I thought I could not treat and old man so and so I started for home with my two little girls. I trotted all the way except when near the gate and near the brige but could not see the horse except when a flash of lightning came. I thought I never was so thankful for God's Eleghant brilliant lightning as I was then for I could not see my hand only when it shined so splendid. I was not the least affraid. I felt that I was in Gods hand so mighty and able to guard me safe from every ill. How wonderful is his Goodness. Came home all safe before the rain. Had hard rain and thunder in the night. Arose once and looked toward the barn to see if it was struck with the lightning.

June 22 was written first before 21

June 23 [22] wednesday

Nice day. Very busy. Acksy Perine called. Was very glad to see her.

June 24 [23] Thursday

Very busy and very tired.

June 25 [24] friday

Tillie and con called. I was very busy doing house work and making the children dresses.

June 26 [25] Saturday

Very busy fixing for Mr Reid to come home. The children went to freehold for him but he did not come.

June 27 [26] Sabbeth

Did not go to church. Had no one to drive and tie the horse. Mr Clayton went away in the morning.

June 28 [27] Monday

The children went after Mr Reid to freehold station and came back with Elwood and their Father about eleven oclock. I was very glad to see him home safe.

June 29 [28] Tuesday

Mr Reid was taken about twelve oclock with a bad diareah. I gave him all I had in the house but did not help him. About five in the morning he threw up and was taken with cranps in his limbs. I worked with all my might until nine oclock in the morning when the Dr came. He was then very bad but the Dr said the worst was over. I put his feet in warm bath twice and put on mustard plaster and rubbed him with wells linament[193] for the cranps but he was like a dead man until two oclock when he rallyed and was better and I had had the comfort to see him in comfort. The Doc could not find his pulse when he came.[194] This God is the God we adore. Our Faithful unchangable friend whose love is as great as his power and nether knows measure. It was a very sad day long to be remembered.

June 30 [29] Wednesday

Mr Reid a little better. John a native of Rusia lived at Charly Jewells and came and set up with him and let me rest and took such good care of him all night. I slept but little but had a good rest.

July 1 [Friday]

Mr Reid but little better and I very tired.

[193] Wells liniment: a commercial remedy, a salve.

[194] William Reid was probably suffering from gastro-enteritis from contaminated food. His cramps and weakness may have been due to the loss of potassium and water resulting from the diarrhea and vomiting. His faint pulse and slow recovery may have resulted from unrelieved dehydration. William was extremely ill and was home most of July recuperating.

July 2 [Saturday]

Very little better and I so wore out I can hardly keep about.

July 3 [Sunday]

A little better. Tillie and Con came and the children staid all night.

July 4 [Monday]

A nice day. Elwood took Lizzie and Florence to the old church to a festival and had a nice time.[195]

July 5 [Tuesday]

A nice day. Tillie and Con came home and helped Mr Reid get hay. He is very weak but gets arround.

July 6 Wednesday

Nice day. Was very busy ironing. Very tired.

July 7 Thursday

Very busy baking and so tired can scarcely keep about.

July 8 friday

Very busy Ironing and cooking goosberies. Mr Reid took me to aunt margarets and took tea with her. Called as we came home to see aunt harriet. She is sick with erieyples [erysipelas] in her arms.[196] Lizzie and Florence kept house.

July 9 Saturday

Mrs Macky came and cleaned the citchen floor for me.

July 10 Sabbeth

Oh the wonderful goodness of God in providing a day of rest. Nothing but an all wise being could see how man needed a day of rest and quiet, so sweet and refreshing. Mr Reid and lizzie went to church. Elwood went the night before to

---

[195] The children probably went to the festival given that day at the Freehold Methodist Church. This was a fund-raising event given by the women of the church in conjunction with July Fourth patriotic observances. Elwood may have been attracted by the musical events for, according to the *Monmouth Democrat* of July 7, 1870, "The choir of the church, and the amateur glee club performed several choice pieces of music at intervals, in excellent style."

[196] Erysipelas: a streptococcal infection causing severe inflammation of the skin.

see Johny Reid. Florence and myself prepared dinner and in the afternoon the children went to sabbeth school.

July 11 Monday

Nice day. Had a splendid shower in the night.

July 12 Tuesday

Nice day. Had a lovely rain in the night and evening.

July 30

Nice day. I have been very busy and not very able to work and it has been very warm weather. Con and tillie came home and Garret Denice and Virginia and I was so glad to see them. They took dinner with us and went after huckle berries.

July 31

Nice day. Cooked dinner for uncle Joseph Reid[197] but he did not come. Looked for him two or three days. Lizzie & Florance went to freehold to fetch home Elwood. Came about eleven oclock.

August 1 [July 31] Sabbeth

A lovely day. Went to church with mr Reid. Came home done the dinner work. Mr Cob preached a very smart sermon on horse racing the best I ever herd on the sui ʻect.
  Howard and Elijah Reid took tea with us.

August 2 [1] Monday

Went with Mr Reid and the children and took dinner with cousin Elijah Reid. Had a very nice time. Came home about five oclock.

August 3 [2] Tuesday

I was very busy. Mr Reid went in the afternoon after a girl for me. I had been sick all night and day. Came home with the girl a bout dusk.

August 4 [3] Wednesday

Lizzie took Mr Reid to freehold to go to new york in the morning but the cars had left. I was so sorry to have him go it is so warm and sickly in new york. If he could have stayed home a couple of weeks more it would not have been so warm.
  I felt so bad about his going I could not sleep. I felt as if some thing had hap-

---

[197] Possibly Joseph I. Reid: William Reid's uncle, his father's brother.

pened. It is so sad to have him go away from his comfortable home to make a living among strangers. If his father could see from the land of rest where I hope he has gone what his injustice has done to make some sons rich and crush some down with no help which he was so able to give and never would have felt it. All the wagon he ever gave him when he went to farming was worn out when he gave it to him. He gave four of his sons farms and gave him but two thousand altogether cattle and all the same that he gave his girls.

August 5 [4] Thursday

A dull showery day. Went to take Mrs Renlue some butter. I feel a little better to day but am very sad about Mr Reid but my hope is in God. He is so good and kind and can take care of all we trust to him. He never will forsake us the goodness. What should I do with my burden of care if I had no kind wonderful God to go to with so many of my dear ones gone away from me? Wonder goodness to take care of all my dear ones at once and the same time and they so far apart, and can never pay him for it. Nothing but thanks can I ever give.

August 6 [5] Friday

Nice day. Aunt Margaret took dinner with me and uncle Bennie also. Had a very nice time, but am so weak to work all day, I get very little leisure. My sewing is so much ahead of me. A splendid moon light evening.

August 7 [6] Saturday

A very warm day. Very busy baking. Went to freehold in the afternoon and goot me a parasol and some muslin. Come home about dusk. Sold some chickens in the morning. A very splendid moon light night.

August 8 [7] Sabbeth

A very beautiful morning. Arose early. Wanted so much to go to church. It was communion and I was ready early but the horse was not harnesed soon enough and it was too late to go. I was so sorry. The girl went home in the afternoon. Elwood came home to dinner. A beautiful moon light night.

August 9 [8] Monday

A very splendid morning. Went to freehold to take Elwood to freehold. Had a splendid ride. Went to Mrs Bentues for becky Bentu to do house work. She came.

August 9 Tuesday

A dull morning. Becky washed and worked very smart. I sewed some and Ironed some. Busy all day. Wet my flowers by moon light and set out one flower in my mound. It is a splendid night. The catydids are singing and the children is sitting out doors telling stories and I am writing with a musketoe around my ears bussing and biting by turns, and now I am going to read some in my bible and have prayers and go to bed, and such a kind heavenly father to take care of me and all my dear ones where ever they are. Such an all seeing God what would we do without his watchful care and all with such a tender hand. I feel as if no evil could come where Gods eye was and I know it is every where beholding the evil and the good.

August 10 wensday

A nice day. Had a nice rain in the night. All well. Sewed the most of the day. Had a splendid rain in the afternoon. *I went out and was caught in it and drove in west Bucks wagon house.*[198]

August 11 Thursday

A very showery day. Aunt susan staid all night with me and cousin Davy Applegate also. Was very glad of their company for I am so lonesome at night that I am very thankful for the company of a friend.

August 12 friday

A very nice day. Went with Lizzie & Florance to Garret Denices and spent the day with virginia. Had a splendid time. Every thing tasted lovely & I made Lizzie a white skirt on her sewing machean.

August 13 Saturday

A very stormy day. Jimmy Shepherd cut some wood for me and hoed some and done some work out in the rain for me. In the evening Cab and Elijah Reid called and staid all night. Cab went to Freehold for Elwood.

August 14 Sabbeth

A very rainy day. Cleared off in the afternoon. Cab and Elijah & Elwood went out in the afternoon.

August 15 Monday

Nice day. Becky came in the morning and Elwood went to Tillies. I was sick with soar throat and head ache contracted going out in the rain.

August 22 [25] Thursday

Went to Tillies and took her some peaches.

---

[198] Possibly a wagon shed belonging to Sylvester Buck, a neighbor on the main road to Freehold.

August 24 [27] saturday

Tillie and Con spent the day with us.

August 28 [31] Wensday

Went to see Daniel Laird a cousin of my Mothers. He is very sick.

August 30 [September 2] friday

Went to Tillies to take her some peaches and brought Lizzie to John Reids. Came home about dusk and found Mr Reid home. I was very glad. I feel very safe when he is home.

Sept 1 [3] Saturday

Very busy baking in the morning and pickeled pears in the afternoon. Very tired at night.

Sept 2 [4] Sabbeth

Went to church with Mr Reid. Herd Mr Cobb preach. Had a nice shower when we came out of church. Was sick all the afternoon and night. Very weak in the morning.

Sept 3 [5] Monday

Very sick and weak in the morning but a little better in the afternoon. Went with Mr Reid to the station at freehold and got me a dozen glass cans two quart cans [199] for three dollars and went to John reids for Lizzie. Had a very dusty ride.

Sept 4 [6] tuesday

A lovely day. Very busy canning and washing and went to Mr Irones store[200] in the afternoon late and called on aunt Margaret. Come home by moon light. Very sweet ride.

Sept 5 [7] Wednesday

Nice day. Very busy making pies and two kinds cake for the sabbeth school picknick.

Sept 6 [8] Thursday

A cool lovely day. Arose very early and got ready for the pick nick. Spent it delightfully with the Mounts corner school and the freehold baptist school.

[199] Glass canning jars.

[200] Gilbert H. Irons: a retail merchant whose store was located at Clayton's Corners.

Florence came home with a soar throat and head ache. Herd of a dreadful axident. A brige broke and let a car load of children in the river eight feet under water and thirty dead and missing. It happened towards the shore. I made a mistake. It was not the cars but they where marching teachers & schollars over an old brige over the river when the brige gave way and brige and all went down in very deep water.[201] We had three schools with the Tompson Grove. It was a mixed picknick made up of baptist & methodist and prespetarian and all passed off so well and agreeable and such a plentiful entertainment.

Sept 7 [9] Friday

A nice morning but Florrene has had a roasting fever all night and I have slept but little. She has a bad soar throat I have docttored her up as well as I [can]. I was busy as usual. Ironed in forenoon and caned peaches in the afternoon and sewed a little. Had a splendid moon light night.

Sept 8 [10] Saturday

A very dull morning and cloudy several times through the day intersperced with sunshine. Florance so much better that she arose and dressed for breackfast. I was very busy baking in the morning and caned nine quarts peaches in the afternoon. Lizzie went to freehold for her brother Elwood just at night. I expect him home with her about ten or eleven oclock. What a glorious thing that there is a rest above for the weary & heavy laden. I often think of that home in the skies Glorious home in the skies where the wicked cease from troubling and the weary are at rest. A home purches by the dear dear Saviour for us so unworthy.

Sept 9 [11] Sabbeth

A cool lovely morning. Elwood took me to church and I herd Mr Cobb preach a very good sermon. He seemed much affected about the death of Sherreff Perine[202] a wealthy man with no children and never served the dear Saviour. If he had loved the dear saviour Mr Cobb would not have felt so badly. We can see when it is too late what we might have done for his soul, but all is

---

[201] The tragedy Sarah writes about occurred in Toms River on September 8, 1870. According to the *Toms River Courier*, September 16, 1870, a large group of children and adults from Long Branch arrived by train at Toms River to attend a Methodist Sunday School outing. To reach the village from the depot the crowd had to cross a long, narrow foot bridge over the river. The bridge collapsed under the weight of the crowd, plunging people into the water below. During the panic that ensued eight people were drowned, adults and teenagers, all from Long Branch. A full article on the tragedy appeared in the *Monmouth Democrat*, September 15, 1870.

[202] John M. Perrine: was elected sheriff of Monmouth County in 1831. He died on September 5, 1870 in Manalapan.

over now. Oh dear saviour help me to be faithful to the souls arround me, that I may be the means of them to that glorious home in the skies.

Sept 10 [12] Monday

A very cool morning but a lovely day. Very busy. Lizzie took Elwood to free-hold and came back half past eight & went with florance to school. I help wash and preserved six lb of peaches & pickeled some two jars & caned two cans besides other work. Very tired to night. I am so glad there is a land of rest. I am so thankful that Jesus has perchased a glorious home for all who will believe on him so free without money or price.

Sept 14 wednesday

A splendid day but very dusty. We went to the fair. Charly Jewell drove for us. We had a nice time. Saw President Grant and had a nice fair.[203] Saw Elwood and came home early and mised our dog. We thought so much of him.

Sep 15 Thursday

A nice day. Very busy. Becky did not come until late and I cooked some quinces in the afternoon. Went to Mr Bearmores and to Mr Gravats for my turkeys in the afternoon near sundown.

Sept 16 friday

A very nice day. Busy sewing and doing house work.

Sept 17 Saturday

I was disapointed when I arose in the morning and found it had been raining. I was a going to Aarons that is mr Reids brother and Miss Bert [204] was going with me. It proved to be a very stormy day and we had no wood cut for a storm. I thought Mr Reid would come home and he came through the storm. We was very glad to see him home once more and we was so lonesome in the storm.

---

[203] During the Seventeenth Annual Monmouth County Fair, on September 14, 1870, President Ulysses S. Grant visited Freehold. His visit was well-publicized and large crowds came to the fair that day. The President arrived around 10 o'clock in the morning and went to the residence of former governor Joel Parker where a reception was held. He then went in Parker's carriage to the fair grounds where he toured the exhibits and attended the races. Later in the afternoon the party went to the American Hotel for an elaborate dinner and numerous speeches. The President drove in his carriage back to the Cottage-by-the-Sea, his summer residence in Long Branch, after dinner.

[204] Hester E Burtt: the fiancee of Spafford Reid, William Reid's nephew, the son of his younger brother John H. Reid. Spafford and Hester were married on November 4, 1869.

Sept 18 Sabbeth

A very dull morning. Mr Reid had no clothes home with him to go to church, and he went to see his daughter Tillie, and I accompanied him.

Sept 19 Monday

We all arose before four oclock and Lizzie went with her Father to Freehold to fetch the horse and buggy home and I went with Tillies two little girls to uncle Gilberts and had a splendid time. Saw Elen Jewell and Tillie Preston. Did not get started for home until after sun down. Arived home safe before it was very dark.

Sept 20 Tuesday

An uncommon busy day. We washed and baked and had time to set out my bed of tulips and went to the peach orcherd and got some peaches with little Fannie & Lizzie.

Sep 21 wednesday

Nice day. Went to Tillies and took little Lizzie[205] and Florence along with me. Little Lizzie had a soar throat. Staid all night with Tillie.

Sep 22 Thursday

A very cool morning. Con took Tillie and me to the fair at Trenton.[206] We had a splendid ride. Saw Mr James English[207] & bought some flower bulbs that I prize very much.

Sept 23 friday

Came home by uncle Gilberts and Margaret Alice came home with me. Arived home about three oclock, found all safe and well but Fannie had the soar throat.

Sep 24 Saturday

Nice day. Very busy Ironing and baking & doing Saturday work all day and went to freehold in the evening and saw Mary Reid cousin Williams wife and daughter lizzie.

Sep 25 Sabbeth

I was not well. I was so tired I could not rest all night and such a bad pain in

---

[205] Lizzie: Sarah's three year-old granddaughter.

[206] The fair of the Central Agricultural Society of New Jersey was held from September 20-22, 1870. The Reids would have taken the train, a rare adventure.

[207] James English: a prosperous farmer in Manalapan.

my back. I had a sweet day of rest. Oh it is so good in God to give us a day of holy rest. He knew we would need it so much.

Sep 26 Monday

Rebeckah did not come and I had the work to do so I was very busy. I went for her in the evening and she came.

Sep 27 Tuesday

Nice morning. David Applegate came for Margaret alice. His mother was sick. I was so sorry to have her go home. She was coming so long and must go home so soon. Cleaned three fish in the forenoon and went to Mr Irones for salt.

Sep 28 Wednesday

Nice day. Washed in the morning and went to blacks mill to hear from aunt susan she is very sick.

Sep 29 Thursday

Nice day. I washed some in the morning and went to see aunt susan. Started about a quarter of eleven and came home at four oclock. Aunt susan is no worse the doctor says.

Sep 30 friday

A very stormy day. We was so lonesome in the storm. I was ironing and had a bad head ache and very little wood cut. I was looking for Mr Reid home all day. He did not come in the morning and did not come in the five oclock train. We went to bed early I had such a bad head ache, and Mr Reid came in the eight oclock train. We was so glad to see him.

Oct 1 Saturday

Nice day. A little dull in the morning. We had the pleasure of the company of Cora Smith William smiths daughter.[208] The children had a nice time playing with her. She seems to be a very sweet child. The children went for elwood in the evening.

Oct 2 Sabbeth

A nice day. Mr Reid had no clothes with him to go to church. We had a nice time at home. The children and Rebecca went to sabbeth school. We had Elwood home until afternoon.

---

[208] William M. Smith: the owner of the store at Smithburg village.

Oct 3 Monday

A stormy morning. Mr Reid went to New York in the afternoon. I sewed
some on the children sacks.

Oct 4 Tuesday

A nice morning. I was very busy baking and washing. My turkeys came home
from Mr Parkers. They have been there two weeks and they have lost but one
turkey and several chickens. I think I have done well to get them home any
how. They have been hunted all over for, and could not find them.

Oct 5 Wednesday

A splendid day. We cleaned two pantries in the morning. Elwood went to the
woods to get a load of wood.

Aunt margaret and uncle Bennie came in the afternoon and Mrs Perine came
to wards night. I was very glad to see them all. Had a nice time but too very
short. The afternoons is altogether too short to pay a visit just at night.

Oct 6 Thursday

A very dull stormy and blowey day. The children did not go to school. Lizzie
and me cleaned a bed room. Elwood went to see Tillie in the morning.

Oct 7 friday

A dull morning. Elwood came home in the morning. I done my Ironing in
the morning, and took up my flower roots in the afternoon.

Oct 8 Saturday

A splendid day. Very lovely like a summers day. I done Saturdays work and
cleaned a bed room and caned two cans of pears. I am very tired to night. It is a
sweet lovely moonlight night and my work is done for this day, and the sweet
sabbeth of rest will dawn in a few hours and I shall be so glad to have a rest so
sweet and a nice time to read, but I have no one to drive to church so I will
have to stay home, but God is every where. Oh the wonderful goodness of god to
let us call upon his great name as often as we will.

Oct 9 Sabbeth

A lovely day. Rebecca went home ear[ly] about sunrise I arose very soon and
prepared breckfast. My two littl girls done the work that was to do out doors.
Had a very happy day. Lizzie went to sabbeth school and florence did not want
to go. She had not read her library. In the evening Charly Jewell called and
fetched a letter from my housband. I am very glad to see him. We was very lonesome at ight. It was a splendid night as light as moonlight can be. We wrode
down in the dusk of evening and saw aunt margaret a minute.

Oct 10 Monday

A splendid day. Rebecca came early and we washed and done house work. I went all over the fields to find a hog that we missed and found it in the corn-field. In the evening wrote to mr Reid. Very tired when done.

Oct 11 Tuesday

A dull day. Rained about one oclock a little. Rebecca and myself cleaned the citchen. I wight washed it nearly three times over and am very tired to night but it is a great satisfaction to have it over and gone.

Oh to be prepared for that land of rest where the wicked cease from troubling and the weary are at rest to have ones work well done at last and a place at Jesus feet. It appears to me I should never want to move from that spot if I can ever reach that Glorious place and see saviour's face although so unworthy. Yet he has died for the chief of sinners the chief so I may find a place if my service has been ever so poor.

Oct 12 Wednesday

A very rainy morning. I was almost sick, the result of my yesterday. I work with a dull head ache, and I can scarcely wright for Lizzies tongue. She is so very impudent to me. This forenoon I was worried almost sick. Lizzie and Florrence would go to school in the rain. All I could say they would not give up, at last I told them they could if it stoped raining, but they would not wait untill it stoped. It rained hard until they walked a mile and was soaking wet when they got there. I never was so tried with two children in my life. Lizzie is the most headstrong child ever was raised. I baked in the morning and sewed in the after-noon and uncle Gill called with Lizzie in the morning.

Oct 13 Thursday

A nice day. The children went to school. I did not work very hard. I Ironed some. Went to aunt margarets in the afternoon. Saw Miss Bert there. Came home and went with the children to Charly Jewells to see Annie Jewell my cousin.

Oct 14 friday

Nice day. Went to Mr James Parkers[209] for my turkeys and brought them home. Very tired. Sewed some. Mended shirts.

Oct 15 Saturday

Nice day. Baked in the morning. Was very busy churning and Saturday work.

---

[209] James Parker: a nearby neighbor on the main road to Freehold.

Had the pleasure of Miss Berts & aunt margarets company in the afternoon.
Went in the evening to freehold to fetch Elwood home. We arived home half
past ten in the evening.

Oct 16 Sabbeth

Splendid morning. Had a hard time to get Elwood to go to meeting with me.
He went but did not want too. It is the second time he has took me to church
this summer and then he was not willing to go but I got there and herd a splendid sermon on charity. Mr Cob gave us a lovely sermon. It was better than any
four sermons I ever herd on the subject. Tillie came in the fournoon and the little children.

Oct 17 Monday

A dull morning. I went after brectfast to Mr Perines after my turkey and
brought them home and after dinner I went with rebecca to Mr Parkers for some
turkeys. They are the worst turkeys I ever had and in the afternoon just at night
I went to Mr Mcglockens[210] to fetch home an old turkey that run away. Came
home very tired. Had a beautiful sunset.

Goodness and mercy has followed me all the days of my life and I hope to
dwell in the house of the Lord forever.

Oct 18 Tuesday

A very blusterday day. The wind blew a huracane almost. I went to the woods
to get some white oak for tea for my turkeys, and then went to the nut trees for
nuts. In the afternoon sewed some. Went to aunt margarets and uncle Bennie.
Went for Mr Reids letter but it did not come.

Oct 19 Wednesday

A very nice day. I was very busy baking in the forenoon. In the afternoon I
had the company of Miss Lizzie Clayton & Johanna. I was so glad to see them.
They are such pleasant nice girls. It is a very cold night. We like the fire to
night. A cold room feels chilly. I feel anxious about Mr Reid. I have not [heard]
in more than a week. The pope is a potentate no longer. Feb 16=1870 The king
of Itily took possesion of Rome. The Kings name is Victor Emanuel.[211]

Oct 20 Thursday

A very stormy day. It rained hard in the afternoon. Lizzie was very wet helping Recbea [Rebecca] put up the horses. It was very gloomy. I looked for Mr Reid
home but he did not come.

---

[210] Thomas McGlocken: an nearby neighbor.

[211] Sarah is noting the annexation of Rome, the final step in the unification of Italy under King Victor
Emmanuel II. An event she may have read about in the *New York Observer*.

Oct 21 Friday

A nice day. Went with aunt margaret to freehold and saw Elwood. Bought some things from him.

Oct 22 Saturday

A nice day. Lizzie Florence & me cleaned the parlor and beckky went away and left me to do the Saturday work to do and I was almost sick.

Oct 23 Sabbeth

A nice day. The children and myself had all the cattle and horses and hogs to feed and milking to do. We could not get ready for church in time but I read a splendid sermon preached in one of the new york churches. Dr Ormistons introductory sermon to his new charge Collegiate Reformed Duch Church. A most splendid sermon.

Oct 24 Monday

A nice day. The children helped me do my work. I was almost sick since Saturday.

Oct 25 Tuesday

A nice day. I baked and helped the children churn and was not able to work and was sick with my back and shoulders and breasts. I was so much between my shoulders that I feel as if I would never see another well day.

God is so wonderful good he has often raised me up almost from the dead. I had a wakeful night. Had a letter from my husband. Was so glad to hear from him. He is making six dollars a day but we do need him so much at home this time of year.

Oct 26 Wednesday

Nice day. I am not able to do any thing so weak in my lungs and between my shoulders. Had a restless night. All my fourty turkeys is dying. I have done all I could to cure them but they will die.

Oct 27 Thursday

A very dull cloudy day. Rains some. We are all alone. Florence has been for Rebecca and she would not come. It is very gloomy but I know my Heavenly Father raing[reigns] and doeth his will in the armies of heaven and among the in habitants of earth and I am so glad that he rules and reigns. I glory in his greatness and goodnes. Nothing can happen but what he wills for our good and his glory and that is enough for me. I rejoice that he reigns forever more.

I baked in the morning and sewed
in the afternoon and uncle Gill called
with Lizzie in the evening.

                      Sarah T Reid

Oct 13 Thursday

a nice day the children went to
school I did not work very hard I
Ironed some went to aunt Margards
in the afternoon saw Miss Bert there
came home and went with the
children to Charly Jewells to see Annie
Jewells my cousin

Oct 14 friday

nice day went to Mr James Flawkers
for my Turkeys and brought them home
very tired Sewed some mended shirts

Oct 15 Saturday

nice day baked in the Morning
was very busy churning and saturdays
work had the pleasure of Miss Berts &
aunt Margarets company in the afternoon
went in the evening to freehold to
fetch Elwood home we arived home
half past ten in the evening.

Oct 16 Sabbath

splendid Morning had a hard time
to get Elwood to go to meeting with me
he went but did not want too it is
the second time he has took me to
Church this Summer and then he was
not willing to go but I got there and
herd a Splendid sermon on charity
Mr Cob gave us a lovely sermon it was
better than any four sermons I ever
herd on the subject. Tillie came in
the sickroom and the little AirHaven

Oct 17 Monday

a dull morning I went after
breakfast to Mr Spences after my Turkeys
and brought them home and after
dinner I went with rebecca to Mr
Parkers for some Turkeys they are the
worst Turkeys I ever had, and in
the afternoon just at night I went to
Mr Mcglockens to fetch home an old
Turkey that run away, came home very
tired, had a beautiful sun set,

goodness and mercy has followed
me all the days of my life and I
hope to dwell in the house of the
Lord forever,

Sarah T Reid

Oct 18 Tuesday

a very blusterday day the wind
blew a huracane almost, I went to the
woods to get some white oak for tea
for my Turkeys, and then went to
the nut trees for nuts, in the afternoon
sewed some, went to aunt Margarets
and uncle Bennie went for Mr Reids
letter but it did not come,

Oct 19 wednesday

a very nice day I was very
busy baking in the forenoon, in
the afternoon I had the company
of Miss Tizzie Clayton & Johanna
I was so glad to see them they are
such pleasant nice girls, it is
a very cold night we like the fire to
nights a cold noon feels chilly
I feel anxious about Mr Reid I
have not in more than a week

Oct 28 Friday

Nice day. Uncle Bennie was here to dig potatoes and stayed to dinner with us. I was not able to do any house work. Sewed some on Florrences sack and finished it and my lungs was worse all night. Could not sleep such a weak bad feeling in my lungs. How frail is life. A little too much work and I am distressed for breath and can scarcely talk. Oh for a home above the skies where sicknes never comes. I wanted so much to go and see a sick man this week that is near his end. I am so sorry I could not go. I wanted to tel him how ready Jesus is to forgive all our sins.

Oct 29 Saturday

Cold and windy. Aunt margaret called. Lizzie has gone to freehold for Elwood & Florrence is doing the night work out doors. It is too bad for a little girl to milk and feed hogs and wood and every thing.

Oct 30 Sabbeth

A nice day. Was not well enough to go to church. I had a nice time reading and read a splendid peace in the observer [New York Observer] about Eusabius[212] visit to Jerusalem and the mount of olive where his dear feet last pressed the earth. How I should like to stand on that mount. What a great privalege to be able to go there. Commenced to rain hard four oclock.

Oct 31 Monday

A very cool morning. Had a very stormy night. I did not sleep much. Was so uneasy about the horses being out in the rain and my turkers out in it. It was a very windy day. Elwood went to freehold in the afternoon and lizzie brought the horse home.

Nov 1 Tuesday

A cool lovely day. I was able to do some little shores arround the house. It is such a pleasure to be able to work for my children. Tillie was home with little lizzie. I was so glad to see her. Lizzie took up my tube rose roots this afternoon and Gladiolas also. I have been several days reading My Fathers House.[213] It is the most sublime and Eleghant language I ever read. I am so rejoiced with it, it is a perfect feast.

---

[212] The *New York Observer* carried "Around the World," the letters of "Eusebius,"as a regular feature of its foreign coverage. The original Eusebius of Caesaria was a fourth-century theologian.

[213] James Madison MacDonald, *My Father's House; or, The Heaven of the Bible*, a book of consolation (Philadelphia: Bradley & Co., 1869) was written by a Presbyterian clergyman and published in New York in 1855. Several editions followed with the last edition appearing in 1869. MacDonald was the author of several books on religious subjects. This book provided an elaborate description of the glories of heaven, what life there would be like, and who would be there.

Nov 2 Wednesday

Mrs Mack washed for me. I sewed some in the afternoon. Very nice day. Lizzie & Florance went to mr Smocks [214] to spend the night. Sallie Gravat came in the afternoon and staid all night with me. She is a nice girl.

Nov 3 Thursday

A cool day. Mrs Mack mixed bread for me and Sallie helped me bake and do house work. Lizzie came home with Florance in the afternoon.

Nov 4 Friday

A nice day. The children and myself was alone and we saw Mr Reid comming home. We did not expect him and we was so glad to see him.

Nov 5 Saturday

A nice day. Mr Reid and uncle Bennie got up our stocks, and Mrs Mack ironed for me. I was very tired at night and so glad God had made a day of rest the sweet rest of the sabbeth day.

> Oh for a heart to prais my God
> A heart from sin set free
> A heart that always feels thy blood
> So freely shed for me.

Nov 6 Sabbeth

A lovely morning. I was not able to go to church. Elwood came home & Jake Appelgate with him and Tillie and Con was home. I was glad to see my children home. It is one of the bright spots of earth to have our dear ones arround us.

Nov 7 Monday

A nice day. The cars left Mr Reid in the morning and in the afternoon I went with him to Englishtown station[215] and then drove to the saw mill[216] for a girl but did not get any one. Came home about dusk and Florrance had broken my white wash bowl that belonged to my room. I was so sorry I could have cried if it would have done any good.

Nov 8 Tuesday

A nice day. A little windy but a lovely day. I swept some in the yard. Mr Perine was here and brought us three barrels of appels at fourteen shillings a bar-

---

[214] Possibly A. A. Smock: owner of a home on the way to Blacks Mills.

[215] Englishtown was one of the stops on the Freehold & Jamesburg Agricultural Railroad.

[216] Sarah may have driven to the saw mill on Pine Brook, owned at the time by Charles Van Cleaf.

rel. It is a splendid moon light night. The children has done the night work and all well.

Nov 9 Wednesday

A dull morning. I went to Mrs Johnson to pay her the ballence of Rebeccas wages and see her about a very wicked untruth she had told about Elwood. She acknolleged she had told what was false but did not know why she told it. We had a storm in the afternoon and night. It is very gloomy in a storm without Mr Reid home if it was not for my strong hope in a God that is always near and arround us. Oh what a good and wonderful glorious help in ervy time of need and a strong and kind friend ever near and knows our ervy wish and we have only to ask and we have all we ask for and more than we could ask.

Nov 10 Thursday

A cold blowey morning. I went to bring the cows up to milk. Lizzie said she would not go. We had a lovely time all alone me and my two little girls. They done nearly all the work. Lizzie done the out doors work. They do not want me to do any thing. I am getting stronger but am not a giant cuite. In the evening Mr West buck called and brought home a horse he had had to work for its keeping. We was a little startled to hear some one at the barn saying wo to the horses but our sporty would not let him come in the gate until I caled him away.

Nov 11 Friday

A cold morning but it was cuite warm in the afternoon. The children and myself went to freehold and had their hats trimmed at Miss weeds. Came home about dark.

Nov 12 Saturday

A cool morning. Very busy doing housework. Lizzie went to freehold for Elwood, and James Johnson came here to cut wood a little in lickor and it made me almost sick to have a man around that had been drinking. It made me feel cuite nervous. I shall be so glad to have mr Reid home once more to stay. We do need him so much, but Elwood will be home in an hour or two.

Nov 13 Sabbeth

A lovely day. I wanted Elwood to take the children to church but he was not willing. He wanted to stay home. I had some time to read and it was very a great privalige.

Nov 14 Monday

A nice warm morning. Lizzie took Elwood to freehold and I went to English Town for a girl but peter Clayton said I best not go for her I would be sorry if I had any thing to do with them and so I did not go for her, and so I came home without her but such a time as I had when I arived home Lizzie was so much displeased she cried hard as she could but not as loud as she could and then such a blowing as I got and so much impudence it was hard to bear from a child thirteen years old and did not stop until I told her cousin annie was coming and as soon as cousin annie was gone she commenced to storm again, but she is quiet now she has her blow out. I have learned to hear all meekly for I know when Jesus was reviled he reviled not again and I have learned the good lesson not to let little things put me out of temper. I shall be satisfied if I can gain heaven that land of rest through cross and trials what ever my Father thinks best to help me on to heaven. He knows best and not one trial more than is needful will he put uppon me.

Nov 15 Tuesday

A very nice day. Mrs Mack came to wash and she mixed my bread for me and I baked and commenced a cuilted skirt for Lizzie. Spent a very nice day. The setting sun was very eleghant. Words cannot express its beauty evry cloud and wave was shaded with a rosy glow. I feel so thankful that makes earth so beautiful. I went in the wagon house for corn for my turkey and found some one had been taking our corn. As much as a load is gone and three of my turkeys. Would go to mr Parkers and I brout them home and they went away next morning but they say they did not come there which is very unlikely, and so I met with two losses in one day and we need all we have. It made me feel a little sad.

Nov 16 Wednesday

A cool morning. The ice was hard but a lovely sunnie day. I went with Lizzie to freehold and took dinner with matilda Conover and came back and took tea with aunt Margaret and had a nice time.

Nov 17 Thursday

A cool morning. We arose a little before five and I went to tillies and she went with me to hidestown [Hightstown] and I bought Lizzie & Florence and Fannie a dress and was back to tillies at three, and I came home. Stoped at Garret Denice and was home about dusk all safe.

Nov 18 Friday

A little cloudy. I done the house work and Lizzie looked all over the farm for a hog that went away in the night a m and could not find it. I was very much worried about it. I was ironing all the forenoon. In the afternoon mended clothes.

Nov 19 Saturday

A very cold morning. I done the house work. Lizzie went to look in the woods for the hog and Florance went to aunt margarets for uncle Bennie and he came and aunt Margaret with him. We had a very nice time. They stayed to dinner and uncle Bennie found the hog under the barn with nine little pigs. The children was so glad and I was so relieved for I thought we would find her dead some where. In the evening Florance was making her brother a watch case and Lizzie came with a candle and set it down on her work and knocked the candle out on the watch case and spoiled it and never said once she was sorry for it but said she did not care and she did not for there was plenty of room on the table to set the candle without setting it almost in her sisters face. I was very sorry but I could not help it. Lizzie never cares who she discommodes if she is suited.

Nov 20 Sabbeth

A cool lovely morning. I had got cold and had the rhumatism getting my feet damp and was not able to go to church and so I had a lovely time reading the book called My Fathers house and it is splendid. The most sublime language I ever saw in any book exemting the bible. Went just at sundown to Charly Jewells to see him. He came home late Saturday night late and left early Monday morning.

Nov 21 Monday

A lovely day. A little cloudy in the morning. Uncle Bennie came and helped me to kill and pick [pluck] the childrens ducks. Killed twenty five and he took them to the station. Mrs Macky helped me. I have a very lame side and back. Made me almost sick in the morning but I helped until they was all done. God is so good. His goodnes we can not understand or find out. It will take eternity to show forth all his prais and eternity is two short.

Nov 22 Tuesday

Commenced to rain before light in the morning. It continued to rained al day and grew worse towards night. It rained very hard in the evening. I was almost sick all day with the rhumatism, and just as it was poaring down in the evening Mr Reid came in wet as could be. I had looked for him but had given him out.

Nov 23 wednesday

I was so much worse with inflemintory rheumatism that I thought I should be fast in bed in one more night, but God is so wonderful good that Mr Reid brought a bottle of medacine so unexpected that helped me. The first time I tried it I was better. Mr Reid went back to new York in the afternoon. I was so sorry to have him go but his ingagements could not let him stay. Elwood came home after we was in bed.

Nov 24 Thursday Thangksgiving

A nice day. I was a little better. Elwood went to see his cousin Johney, and go a hunting with him. I done some sewing and had a call from cousin Charly Jewell. I was very glad to see him. I have a lonesome time. I cannot move scarsely with out a sharp pain in one joint and a cord drawn up my back so tight I could scarcely move my head and could not get out of bed without almost killing me with pain. Could not get my hands to my feet to put on my shoes.

Nov 25 friday

A lovely day. We was all alone. How good in God to be always so near we can call uppon him in every time of need and that is so often. I feel a great much better than I did last night. Elwood is not home yet. He has been gone two days. I am looking for him home every minute. Florance is almost crying about a tooth she is trying to get lose, and Lizzie has fell and hurt her chest so much she feels very badly. It hurts her to move her armes. Elwood came home.

Nov 26 Saturday

It rained in the night and very dull in the morning but cleared off in the morning. Elwood went to the store in the morning. I was very busy all day. Elwood came home in the evening. I set up until ten oclock to give him his supper and bake him some buckweet cakes but could not keep up any longer.

Nov 27 Sabbeth

A nice lovely morning. I wanted Elwood to take his sisters to church, but his head ached and he did not want to go and I was so sorry. He has always been fixed to go to church and went ever since he was a baby. Now he never wants to go with us and I have no one else to drive, and I think so hard of him for it. I have always been willing to sucrifice any thing almost for his enjoyment with the greatest pleasure, and never have an unpleasant thought about it. That is the difference in a mothers love & a childs.

Nov 28 Monday

A nice morning. Lizzie took Elwood to freehold. I cleaned Elwoods pants and cap. In the afternoon I mended the stair carpet.

Nov 29 Tuesday

A cool splendid day. A lovlier november never saw. I was very busy baking but I could not help looking out and rejoicing that we had such a kind heavenly father that cared so much for us, and the earth he has made so eleghant on a november day. I have the rheumatism yet but have been out doors today see our pigs and the new carryall[217] we got home last week.

Nov 30 Wednesday

A very nice day but not the lovely day yesterday was. It has been a beautiful sunny day. It has been my birth day & would have been a very happy day, notwithstanding I had a severe rheumatic pain in one joint which made me have a sharp pain very often and I worked on all day. Washed windows and done house work and cooked. Mrs Mack was here washing. Lizzie & Florance went to the mill[218] in the buggy and got some hog feed, came home and talked all day about going to singing school. Lizzie gave me no pease becaus I would not say she could sign a dollay. I thought a half quarter was sufficient for a little girl to sign. She went on all day like a tyrant. All the impudince she could think of and every thing she could say to try me. I was tempted to get a whip and give her some of it but I knew a little would not do and I was two busy to spend a long time batling with her. If I had undertaken it I should have kept at it until she felt satisfied. Was sick with pain when I rote this, but God always bears me through and I trust he will until the last. Blessed be his name he has never forsaken me in time of need.

Dec 1 Thursday

I have had a dreadful night. Could not help screaming with the severest pain I ever had. Could not turn in bed or get out without sharp pain and Lizzie had to help me up.[219] Could scarcely stand. I sent Florance over to uncle bennies and they came and aunt Harriet with them, and uncle bennie went for the doctor a little before night and he came. I think I could not have lived until morning if I had not got better. Hannah Gravat staid all night with me and done all she could.

Dec 2 friday

A little easier. The doctor called and aunt margaret & uncle bennie. He has been a good uncle to me all summer. I have trouble him a great deal.

Dec 3 Saturday

A very little better. The children waited on me and done the house work. They had it very hard. Con and Tillie came in the morning & Kate Perine and her mother. I was very glad to see them all.

---

[217] Carryall: a light one-horse carriage, usually four-wheeled, that could carry several people.

[218] Probably the nearby Oakland Mills on the Manalapan River.

[219] Sarah's description of her illness is not detailed enough to indicate what the problem was. It is clear she was over-worked. She sometimes referred to her pain as rheumatism or neuralgia.

Dec 4 Sabbeth

A little better. More comfortable but could not get my back from the chair back without help. Uncle Johny Jewell called in the morning and Elwood came home. Lizzie went to church. Aunt Hariet & aunt Susan called in the afternoon and uncle Gilbert. The children went to freehold to the childrens consert and lost one of my earrings. I had Mrs Applegate little girl to stay with me.

Dec 5 Monday

Nice day. I felt a little better. Mary jane Appelgate helped the children do the house work.

Dec 6 Tuesday

A rainy morning. Con came and killed our beef and Cab Reid came in the morning and helped him with it.

Dec 7 wednesday

Nice day. I sewed the most of the day. The doctor came and vaxinated[220] Lizzie & Florance, & they went to singing school in the evening.

Dec 8 Thursday

Nice day. The children was sick with their arms.[221] They got a little cold I suppose going out. A splendid moonlight night.

Dec 9 friday

A very nice day. I sent for the doctor to see the children. He said they had taken a little cold. It was a splendid moon light night.

Dec 10 Saturday

A cool day. I baked in in the morning and Achia Perine called. We was very glad to see her. Uncle Gil called to get two pigs. Achia went home about seven in the evening. The children went part of the way with her. We enjoyed her company very much. We are expecting Elwood home this evening with Lewis Perine.[222] I am very tired to night and another week is added to the past. Oh for a home in the skies a glorious home in heaven. We had a lovely time singing Gods prais last evening but nothing fills me with joyous extacies as in my young day's why is tis I rejoice so little in any thing. I rejoice more in Gods goodness

---

[220] Vaccinated: There were two procedures for smallpox inoculation at the time. One, called variolation, involved taking matter from an existing inoculation pock and applying it to another person. The other, vaccination, was the Jenner method of barely breaking the skin and applying cowpox vaccine.

[221] Lizzie and Florence were having a reaction to their vaccinations.

[222] Lewis Perrine: the 31year-old son of James W. and Deborah Perrine, neighbors on the main road to Freehold.

than in any thing and the beautiful earth he has made for such unworthy children. Oh for a heart to praise my God a heart from sin set free a heart that always feels thy blood so freely shed for me. I looked for my husband home to night but he has not come. He will soon come home to stay if God takes care of him which I trust he will. It is so wonderful that he can keep all of this earth and the million of worlds of the univers all under the protecting arm and guideing eye with the ease that we could take care of a little kitten. Half past eleven oclock Elwood came in. We was waiting for him. Did not get to bed until twelve oclock. It was a very happy meeting. We was so glad to have him home again. God is so good to us.

11 Sabbeth

A very nice day. The children and my self was not well enough to go out. The children had been vaxinated. We spent a very pleasant sabbeth. Uncle Bennie and cousin Charly called in the afternoon. I had a nice time reading in the book called our Fathers House [My *Father's House*]. It commenced to rain in the night just as Elwood came home. I read one of C's letters and was so much hurt about it that I had a sad heart all the evening.

Dec 12 Monday

It was a very stormy day. Elwood was home all day. Charly Gravat called in the afternoon and took dinner with us.

Dec 13 Tuesday

A nice morning. Mr Johnson went to freehold with Elwood. I finished Florances cuilted skirt and read in the evening in our Fathers house.

Dec 14 wednesday

A nice day. Felt pretty well. Covered a side of a quilt and in the evening cut and sewed carpet rags until bed time. Was very tired and Lizzie & Florance was sick with their arms.

Dec 15 Thursday

A cold winday day. The children was not well. Lizzie had a fever and head ache all day. The doctor called in the afternoon and left her some medacine. Mrs Mack washed for me and did not get any thing hung up. To day it is a very cold blowing night. I would be so glad to have our little family all home this cold night. What many comforts our heavenly Father has prepared for us. I hope my dear husband will soon be home to spend all these cold nights and days. It is such a comfort to have him home I feel is all my care was gone.

Dec 16 Friday

A very blowey day. Mary Jane put the clothes out and got them part dried. I ironed some and wated on the children. They had a bad head ache and fever all night. I kept the fire up and kept some wet clothes on their heads. Got very little sleep and was tired in the morning getting out of bed so much.

Dec 17 Saturday

Nice day. Sent for the doctor. The children had a bad cold, and fever all the afternoon in the night then seemed better.

Dec 18 Sabbeth

A very beautiful day. Florrence was broke out with a rash all over which made me feel very much frightened and almost wild all day. I was all alone with the children. I do not think I ever [. . .] a more unhappy sabbeth. I had no tine to sit down to read for I was waiting on the children and getting meals took all my time. I had no spare moments ever to read in Gods precious world.

Dec 19 Monday

A nice day. The children a little better. Florance was broke out all over. It had spread and was a rednes in the skin almost all over. I was very much worried about her. The doctor called in the afternoon and said it appeared like the scarlot fever but she was getting better. It rained in the night.

Dec 20 Tuesday

The children was better. A nice day but I did not take them down stairs it was so stormy.

Dec 21 wednesday

A nice day. I brought the children down stairs and sewed on Mary Janes dress all the time I could. Elwood came home in the evening. I mean near morning. He sent a darky here for the horse and buggy in the afternoon. After breack Mr Johnson took him to freehold.

A little duch pedler came here and I told him he must wait no longer to receive the saviour. He was a Jew. I told him to read the new testament with the old. I was very busy all day baking bread and mince pies & cake also.

Dec 22 Thursday

Elwood went back to the store. It was a very cold day. I thought Mr Reid would come home in the evening but he did not. I was very busy sewing on Mary Janes dress. The children I baked bread cake and mince pies. Was tired at night.

Dec 23 Friday

Had a snow storm in the night. Very cold. Mr Reid came home in the morning train.[223] We was very glad to see him home safe. I was out to the barn when he came home the first time in a month. I was not looking for him in the morning.

Dec 24 Saturday

A very cold day. I could not keep my feet warm away from the stove. I done house work in the morning. Afternoon I finished Mary Janes dress.

Dec 25 Sabbeth

A nice day. The children was better. Mr Reid staid home from church and we had a nice lovely Sabbeth day. I had a nice time reading in Our Fathers House a lovely book, and the children sing some sweet tunes.

Dec 26 Monday

A nice day. Conover Preston and Tillie & her two little girls spent the day with me. We had a nice time.

Dec 27 Tuesday

A pleasant day. We picked our turkeys and some ducks & Mr Reid sent my geese to New York in a box. They was such beautiful ones I thought so much of them. He bought them for me and paid nine dollars for the three and I have always been so proud of them. They where such beautiful ones. I felt when they went away as if I had not much left. It is very little I have give to me and when I have I prize it so highly that I almost worship it. I had a very sad heart when I found they where going for less than they cost but there was no room for them here.

Dec 28 Wednesday

A snowy day. Mr Reid killed his hogs. I had the neuralgia in my head and arms all the week. I was very busy all day.

Dec 29 Thursday

A beautiful snow. So pure and lovely the most beautiful of earth. I was very busy baking mince pies cake and bread. The children & Mr Reid had a very cold slay ride.

---

[223] Once again William Reid completed his seasonal work in New York City for the year; he remained at home until March 1871.

Dec 30 Friday

A very cold day. Mr Reid & Flora went to english town and came home in a snow storm covered with snow in their faces. Came home about nine oclock.

Dec 31 Saturday

A cold morning. Mr Reid took us all to see tillie. I was covered up head and all. We had a splendid slay ride and plenty of bells.[224] Had a nice visit. They invited us and was looking for us. We had a splendid visit. I would have enjoyed it very much if I had not had a bad head ache all day. We came home after night. It was so warm the slaying was poor in the afternoon, but we had a nice warm ride home about nine when we came in.

Jan 1 Sabbeth 1871

A splendid day. Mr Reid & Elwood went to church. The children was home with me. In the afternoon Elwood went to John Reids, & Mr Reid went over to Charlies to see him, and did not get home until in the evening.

Jan 2 Monday

Sewed some and tried lard.[225] Nice day. Lizzie took Elwood to Freehold.

Jan 3 Tuesday

Cold. Lizzie and Florance went to freehold and got my hat which had been to the miliners all the fall and winter so far. I was not well enough to go out. Mrs Mack washed.

Jan 4 Wednesday

Nice day. Very busy baking. Had company in the afternoon. Davy Appelgate and Lizzie came and we all went to singing school with them and I caught a cold in my throat. Had a very soar throat.

Jan 5 Thursday

Nice morning. Lizzie and David went home. I had a large ironing to do and had a very soar throat.

Jan 6 friday

Very busy ironing and sewed some in the afternoon.

---

[224] Bells on the horse's harness.

[225] Lard was made by "trying" or boiling down hog fat, especially that from the abdomen, to extract the oil, which then hardened into lard. William Reid had butchered his hogs the Wednesday before.

Jan 7 Saturday

A very cold day. Very busy all day. Mended clothes in the afternoon and cooked doughnuts. Sent Elwoods clothes to Mr Perines with Conover preston. I had the rheumatism all day.

Jan 8 Sabbeth

A very cold day. Mr Reid took the children to church and took Lizzie to uncle Gilberts after church. Elwood came home after church. I was very glad to see him. I was very lonesome. A boy was with me but he was not very good company. He took Elwood to freehold after tea.

Jan 9 Monday

Very cold. I mended Mr Reids overcoat & had the rheumatism real bad. Done house work.

Jan 10 Tuesday

A very cold day. Mr Reid went to freehold and I baked bread mince pies and cake and sewed a little on Elwoods shirt.

Jan 11 Wednesday

The cold moderated in the night. It was a very dull day. Mr Reid with three teams and two men filled his ice house all put three load. It is splendid ice about eight inches in thickness. I had the rheumatism and worked all day on my feet. It is pretty hard to work all day in such pain as I have had these two days with no help but little Florance only nine years old but she made a sponge cake yesterday and worked all day like a woman. Done all she could do to help me.

Oh for that heavenly rest my saviour has perchased for me. The chief of sinners not worthy to look towards that heavenly rest. Oh for more love to be swallowed up in love to my dear redeemer who has borne so much for me and borne so with my prone and wandering heart so prone to love the foolish things of earth and love my saviour so little.

Oh for a heart to prais my God
a heart from sin set free
a heart that alway feels thy blood
so freely shed for me.

Jan 12 Thursday

A very warm lovely day like a spring day. It made one feel as if spring was nearer than it is. I felt very thankful to see and enjoy such a lovely sunny day. So good in God to give us such a day in January. I was very busy with none but florance to help me, and such a pain in a rheumatic limb. Dr Freeman called.[226] Aunt Mar spent the day.

Jan 13 friday

A lovely warm day. Mr Reid went for marl early. I done ironing and house work. In the afternoon sewed some. Felt very tired and did not do much in the evening.

Jan 14 Saturday 1871

Quite warm. Very busy. Florance went to Mr Van cleff for some guineas[227] with her Father. Did not get home until after dark. I was reading some in the new observer [New York Observer] and mended clothes until Elwood came home. It was after ten oclock and my eyes hurt me very much. I would like so much to have my evenings to read but it is impossible to get my sewing done with two hands. I stayed home from calling on my neighbors all summer to try to get my sewing done but I cannot without sewing in the time I should have to read. Dear Saviour dwell in my heart and make me love thee more.

Jan 15 Sabbeth

A nice morning. Our people went to church & Florance went and went to uncle Gilberts from church & Lizzie came home with them. In the afternoon Leander Jewell and Kate Reid[228] came and staid all night with us. They are our niece and nephew. I was very glad to see them, & Johny Reid & Clayton called also. I had very little time to read. I wish always to improve my sabbeths, so I may grow in grace and the knollege of our Lord and saviour Jesus Christ.

Jan 16 Monday

A dull day. Leander took Elwood to freehold and spent the day with me and night also. Had a nice time with him & Kate.

Jan 17 Tuesday

A nice cool day. We went with Mr Reid to aunt Margarets and spent the day. Leander & Kate went also. We had a nice time. Came home a little before sundown and fixed to bake. Gods goodness surrounds us. Oh to be nearer my God to thee nearer to thee.

---

[226] Dr. Otis R. Freeman: a local physician with offices on Main Street in Freehold.

[227] Guinea fowl.

[228] Catharine A. Reid: the daughter of William's younger brother, John H. Reid, and Margaret (Dey) Reid.

Jan 18 Wednesday

A nice day. Mr Reid went to Tillies & I was very busy baking, bread mince pies and cake. Lizzie mixed one kind of bread and helped me all she could. I was so sorry just at night she said a very wicked word and I was so sorry so much grieved I would rather she would not have helped me do one thing all day. Oh how I should like my children to serve God. He is so merciful to us and so good. I felt as if I could weep tears of blood if I could lead my dear ones to love the dear saviour.

Jan 19 Thursday

Cool day. I ironed some and Florance & Davy Appelgate & Lizzie came in the evening and staid all night. We was very glad to see them. Florance had a head ache.

Jan 20 friday

I was very busy ironing shirts and collars & was very tired at night and had the rheumatism.

Jan 21 Saturday

I was very busy. Dull day. Ironed some. Went in the afternoon to freehold. Paid Miss Weed for my hat and saw Elwood and bought some muslin of him. Took tallow and eggs.[229] Came home in the evening very dark.

Oh such a busy life. How I long for a sweet rest in that better land but such a wicked hart so taken up with the things that perish. We have a out cast boy that came the night or two before new years in a cold snow storm with poor shoes and clothes and to day he brought two more to stay all night.[230]

Jan 22 Sabbeth

A cold windy morning. Lizzie & her father went to church. Florance had not got clear of her head ache. She had a rheumatic pain in her head. The boys went away after dinner. Elwood came home from freehold church without his breackfast. Clark Perines wife makes a bisness of rushing her breackfast table off of the floor on Sunday mornings to have two clerks that sleep in the store go without any breckfast. I do not thank her. She is a member of Mr Chandler church,[231] but I think she has failed to make it her duty to pracktice the golden rule. My boy never had to go without his breckfast or supper in his life before and no child that I ever had black or white ever went to bed without supper or

---

[229] Eggs and tallow (from the hard fat of beef) were both important farm products Sarah sold in town.

[230] Sarah was accustomed to allowing vagrants to sleep in the barn.

[231] Rev. Frank Chandler (1831-1894), a graduate of Princeton Theological Seminary, was the minister of the Presbyterian Church of Freehold.

went without breackfast. I could not sleep if I had let any one go without their meals as she has repetedly. He had a head ache going until after church and after one oclock.

Jan 23 Monday

A dreadful cold morning. Lizzie went with Elwood to freehold. I was so worried about her driving home such a cold morning but she was soon back. She drove so fast I had not thought of her being more than there when back home and then she went to washing and her and Florance would not let me help her any. They was done by dinner time. We had company to dinner Sam Davison and it was snowing hard and very cold, it was a very cold night.

Jan 24 Tuesday

Very cold. I ironed in the forenoon. In the afternoon Mr Reid and the children went to take a slay ride to thompsons for some guineas and they got them and was back about sundown.

I was all alone. I thought I was alone with God. I love to be alone and God all around. Our greatest friend a friend that stickith closer than a brother.

Jan 25 Wednesday

A cold morning. We had a good coal fire in the sitting room and we all went to tillies and had a nice time. We arived home just after dusk and found the fire burning bright & the room warm. We fetched willie & Fannie home with us.[232] Willie was as warm when we came in as if he had been by a warm stove & did not get any cold.

Jan 26 [Thursday]

Very busy baking. It stormed and snowed all day and all night.

Jan 27 friday 1871

Oh such a splendid snow. The earth so lovely, all pure and bright.

Mr Reid took the children out. They had such a splendid slay ride to the mill to see Mr Gulick about some turkeys.[233] I was alone with little willie and he is so good. I had a nice time, with him.

Jan 28 Saturday

Very cold. Started with Mr Reid to take a slay ride to his brother Joseph and take his sister Matilda along. She was not home and therefore we went to uncle

[232] Sarah's daughter Tillie was approaching the delivery date of her fifth child, so Sarah brought seven-year-old Fannie and Willie, one of the two-year-old twins, to stay with her.
[233] The Gulicks lived near the grist and saw mill known as the Oakland Mills on the Manalapan River.

Gilbert Appelgates to dinner and called on Mrs Gulick and Mr Reid bought three turkeys and came home. Found all safe. The children had had company to dinner their cousins Elijah & Calvin Reid.

Jan 29 Sabbeth

A very cold morning and I wanted so much to go to church but Mr Reid thought he could not get there in time. In the afternoon he went to see tillie.

Jan 30 Monday

Mr Reid took his sister Matilda and myself to see his brother Joseph and Joseph went for a load of marl after we got there. We had a splendid slay ride and lots of bells. All the time I am writing little willie is fumbling with my left hand so I can wright very poorly. He will not stay away from me.

Jan 31 Tuesday

A very dull morning. Mr Reid took the children and made a visit to his cousins Elijah and they came home in the rain. It rained all the afternoon. Willie and me spent a very happy day. My heart felt liter than usual and some sweet verses was running through my head all day.

Feb 1 Wednesday

A nice day. We washed in the morning and had the clothes up before noon. Lizzie done the most of it. I was very tired but done but little of the washing.

Feb 2 Thursday

Very cold morning. I was baking. The children went out to slide and lizzie hurt her back and got cold in her throat. I soaked her feet and gave her some wells linament [Wells Liniment]. All this week is such beautiful moonlights nights. Oh to love my saviour more to be swallowed up in heaven and thee dear saviour nearer to thee nearer to thee my God.

Feb 3 friday

A lovely day. Lizzie had a very soar throat and was sick. Mr Thompson VanCleft and wife took tea with us.

Feb 4 Saturday

Nice day. Mr Reid went to the woods in the afternoon. It was very cold to wards night. Willie had a good cry before going to bed. Could not pleas my husband.

Feb 5 Sabbeth

A very cold morning. Elwood did not get home. I wanted to see him very much.

Feb 6 Monday

Cold weather. Mr Reid is carting marl. Lizzie is a little better. She has a very soar ulcered throat. We have a very busy time to get along without lizzie.

Feb 7 Tuesday

A cold morning. Con came and fetched little Lizzie to stay with us and took fannie home. Tillie had a little daughter Sabbeth morning.[234]

Feb 8 wednesday

Cold day. Mr Reid went twice to the marl pits.

Feb 9 Thursday

Cold day. Very busy sewing on dresses. Florance sick with the soar throat. Lizzie better.

Feb 10 Friday

Nice day. Finished Lizzies dress & florance also. Florance is a little better.

Feb 11 Saturday

A cool morning. Went to see Tillie. Found her mite smart and a nice fat little girl. Miss Ustes went with us. Mr Reid fetched his cow home and a calf a nice calf. We came all the way home on a walk. I was so tired riding so slow and holding little willie on my lap I was sick and such a bad head ache. Elwood and Leonard Reid came a about eleven oclock. I was very glad to see them. We was gone to bed when they came.

Feb 12 Sabbeth

A very stormy morning. Snowed all day. I had a bad head ache all day. Willie is assleep on my lap. I can not write. Elwood & Leonard went away in the evening.

Feb 13 Monday

It snowed all day. We washed and hung our clothes in the chamber.

Feb 14 Tuesday

Nice day a deep snow, and the earth so eleghant. Snow banks all around.

Feb 15 Wednesday

The most lovely brilliant day that earth ever saw. The sun so warm and

---

[234] Tillie and Con's new daughter, Viola Virginia Preston, born on February 5, 1871.

bright and that ervy thing glittering in the bright sun light and almost as warm as a summers day. We was just going to fix for Tillies when James Parker came for the bells and Mr Reid lent them to him. I was very much disapointed but said nothing about it. It was such a lovely day to go.

Feb 16 Thursday

A dull cool morning. Mr Reid & myself went to tillies. Was cuite warm in the afternoon. We came home before night.

Feb 17 friday

A warm morning. Mr Reid took the children to aunt susans and brought her home with him. I was very glad to see her. She was always my best friend when I was a child, and a little orphran she was a mother to me.

Feb 18 Saturday

A nice day. I made doughnuts and buiscuit for dinner, and enjoyed aunt susans company very much. I long dear saviour so much to love thee more.

Feb 19 Sabbeth

A very nice morning. Aunt Susan is here and Tillies little children. I went to church and she took the care of the children. A stranger preached for us. Mr Cob is not well. I was very much disapointed to see a stranger in Mr Cobbs place. I wanted to hear him.

Feb 20 Monday

A nice day. Lizzie done the most of the washing. I helped a little and was sick in the evening and next day could not work. Aunt margaret & uncle Bennie came in the afternoon and aunt Susan went home with them.

Feb 22 [21] Tuesday

A stormy morning. Cleared in the afternoon. Uncle Bennie called & took aunt susan to uncle Johnies.

Feb 23 [22] Wednesday

Con came to see his little ones. They was well, & tillie also.

Feb 24 [23] Thursday

Conover came for his little children. I was very sorry to have them go so soon. They had been here about five weeks and such good pleasant children and willie is such a sweet boy.

Feb 25 [24] friday

A nice day. I was very lonesome. Mr Reid went for marl and I was all alone until almost night & I worked hard blacking stoves and cleaning up. Sewed in the evening.

Feb 26 [25] Saturday

A very warm day. Mr Reid helped me make candles.[235] They made very slow it was so warm, and we herd very sad news. We had an invitation to the funeral of Mrs Preston Cons mother. She had been sick with an inflamation on the lungs but was better so she was up and dressed and died so sudden on friday.

In the midts of life we are in death. Went to freehold in the evening.

Feb 27 [26] Sabbeth

Went to Tillies Elwood & his father. I was home alone all day. It was a stormy day. They came back a little before sundown with Lizzie & Florance Agusta[236] with them. I was glad to see them. They have been gone two days.

Feb 28 [27] Monday

A dull day. We went all of us to Mrs Prestons funeral. There was a great many people out and a very good sermon. Mr Kehu[237] & Mr Cob performed the serveses. I felt very badly. She seemed to be nearer to me than she was. My little granchildren will miss her so much.

Feb 29 [28] Tuesday

A nice day. We washed, and I felt very badly all day about Mrs Preston. I felt so sorry for the girls of hers. I would have gone there if I could.

Feb 30 [March 1] Wensday

I done the work. Went to freehold in the afternoon. Got cards taken.[238]

March 1 [2] Thursday

Nice day. Went to Mrs Perines in the afternoon. They was fixing for Charly Perines wedding.[239]

---

[235] Sarah and William probably made dipped candles using the tallow from their beef.

[236] Sarah calls her daughter Florence by her middle name, Augusta; later she refers to her as Gussie.

[237] Rev. J. L. Kehoo: the minister of the Presbyterian Church of Manalapan.

[238] Sarah may be referring to photographs mounted into cards, or *cartes de visite* a popular form of commercial portrait photography at the time.

[239] Charles C. Perrine and Matilda C. Shepherd were married March 2, 1871 by Rev. Frank Chandler.

Feb 26 Saturday

a very warm day Mr Reid helped me
make candles they made very slow it
was so warm, and we herd very sad
news we had an invitation to the funeral
of Mrs Preston Lous mother she had been
sick with an inflamation on the lungs
but was better so she was up and dressed
and died so Sudden on friday
            in the midts of life we are
in death   went to freehold in the evening

Feb 27 Sabbeth
~~inie~~ they went to Tillies Elwood &
his father I was home alone all day
it was a stormy day they came back
a little before sundown with Lizzie &
Florance Agusta with them I was glad to
see them they have been gone two days

Feb 28 Monday
            a dull day we went all of us
to Mrs Prestons funeral there was a
great many people out and a very good
sermon Mr Re한 & Mr Cob performed the
serveces, I felt very badly she seemed
to be nearer to me than she was, My
little granchildren will miss her so
much

Feb 29 Tuesday
            a ~~stormy~~ a nice day we wash
ed, and I felt very badly all day about
Mrs Preston I felt so sorry for the girls
of hers, I would have gone there if I
could

Feb 30 ~~thurs~~ twesday
~~Lizzie~~ went ~~to school~~ I done the
work   went to freehold in Sarah T Reid

March 2 [3] friday

Very busy ironing & house work. Agusta & lizzie went to school.

March 3 [4] Saturday

A dull stormy day. Mr Reid went to tillies and Lizzie and me baked and done saturdays work. Lizzie worked very smart. She mixed the bread made of the midlings of the weat[240] & swept the chamber also.

March 4 [5] Sabbeth

A nice day. Went with Mr Reid to church and herd Mr Cobb preach.

March 5 [6] Monday

A rainy morning. Mrs & Mr Perine and Acksia spent the evening with us. I was very glad to see them. The visit was very short and espeshily to me. We washed in the morning.

March 6 [7] Tuesday

Gussie and me was all the forenoon doing house work & ironing & watching a woman up the road sitting on the ground a reading a news paper as we supposed, and at last she lay down on the ground, and then we was so worried about her we went to see what was the matter with her, & found a duch woman that could not speak a word of english but hungry and a bad pain by sings [signs] so I brought her home with us and gave her dinner some thing to eat and medacine for her pain. I put her to bed and she had a bad pain when she went to bed and I was not very easy for fear it should prove to be a fever. My granmah took in a sick traveler and next morning he was very sick and it proved to be the yellow fever and he died with it and she almost lost her life with it also, but God rewarded her goodness of heart with a life of eightty seven years, spent in doing good. Her name was Margaret Laird by marrage Reid.[241]

March 7 [8] Wednesday

Made plaster[242] for the woman and gave her medacine. Sewed on Gussies dress.

March 8 [9] Thursday

Ironed some and finished the dress. The duch girl is better and helps me work. Said she wil work for me for five dollars a month.

---

[240] Middlings of the wheat: the coarser parts of the grain, mixed with bran.

[241] Sarah's maternal grandmother.

[242] A mustard plaster.

March 9 [10] friday

A nice day. I went to freehold in the afternoon and left the duch girl and when I came back she was missing and a lot of things gone also among them a nice dress of mine that cost about fourteen dollars. Mr Reid went as soon as he could change his horse and he caught her about twelve oclock. I was very sorry she had had such poor teaching.

March 10 [11] Saturday

A nice day. Was baking and the girl went away after she had washed her cloths and after dinner she went away. I was very sorry for her. I kept thinking all the time my dranmah [grandma's] words who maketh thee to differ. Poor thing if she had been trained right she would not have paid me in the way she did. She cried when she went away and was sorry I think.

Tillie and her babe and Joe Con brought them. I was very much surprised to see them. It was raining and the babe screaming.

March 11 [12] Sabbeth

A very stormy day. The babe had a little cold. I was so glad to have them home. Elwood was home also. It cleared off in the afternon just at night and Con wanted to go to his fathers to spend the night. I was very much opposed to it but dared to say but little I was so much affraid they would take cold.

March 12 [13] Monday

A nice day but windy. We washed and Mr Shepherd & lady and Mrs Crafford & daughter spent the eve with us. Had a very nice time.

March 13 [14] Tuesday

I was all alone doing the house work all day. The children went to school. Very dull weather and rainy.

March 14 [15] Wednesday

Done house work and very dull and rainy weather.

March 15 [16] Thursday

Stormy weather. Very busy.

March 16 [17] friday

Larrence was at work for us. I went to freehold in the afternon. Mr Reid went to newyork.[243] It rained all night.

---

[243] William Reid began his seasonal work in New York City for the year.

March 17 [18] Saturday

Stormy all the forenoon. Cleared off in the afternoon. Mr Reid came home in the eve.

All well.

Aprail 1 saturday

A dull morning. Mr Reid took a load of hay to freehold. Mr Perine helped him load it. Elwood did not come home.

Aprail 2 Sabbeth

It rained all night and had the appearance of a rainy day but cleared off to late for us to getready for church & I was so sorry I wanted to go so much to church. Went in the afternoon to take some things to black Abe. He is sick and so very poor. They both take rum some times that is when they can get it. They was glad to have something nice to eat. I was glad I went. They are so very reched.

Aprail 3 Monday

We washed, that is, Lizzie with Gussies help. I was not very well.

Aprail 4 Tuesday

Lizzie staid home from school and ironed part of the clothes. We wanted to go to freehold but did not.

Aprail 5 Wednesday

Had a load of folks to stay all night. They staid in the barn. They appeared to be dredful poor.[244] The mans name was John Marshal he said he graduated at { . . .] and appeared to be a man of good sence but his whife said he had very poor helth. She had a small child the picture of distress. I could not keep from shedding tears to se the little sufferer. It was almost frose and very little on it. Went to freehold in the afternoon.

Aprail 6 Thursday

Nice day. Ironed Elwoods shirts and went to freehold in the afternoon.

Aprail 7 friday

Very warm nice day. Very busy all day. Had some peas planted in the garden and in the evening Nickles Storms[245] came and a foolish man[246] with him. I was

[244] Once again vagrants stayed overnight at the farm.

[245] Nicholas Storms: a young neighbor.

[246] Foolish: mentally deficient.

so hurt to see him. I have had so many heart aches this week. It appears to me
the sufferings of others casts a shadow over me all this week. As soon as one
object of distress wore off another would take its place, yet how wonderful is
Gods goodness to sinful man. The sight of so much goodness and compashion
fills me with wonder love and prais. If God is for us who can be aghanst us.

Aprail 8 Saturday

A lovely warm day. Very busy baking and so tired. Lizzie went to freehold in
the morning & Mr Reid went in the evening to fetch home Elwood. Lizzie made
ice cream in the afternoon. Here are some lines written by Mrs Scott which I
love so much. I have had them many years.

> I fain would join th' adoring throng
> That around my Saviour stand
> And learn the everlasting song
> Which sounds through the better land
>
> I would lay aside this garb of clay
> For the saints' fine robe of white,
> And speed my flight without delay
>
> To the relms of endless light.
> I would reach my hand to receive the crown
> The christains bright reward;
> And oh! with what joy would I cast it down,
> At the feet of my risen Lord
>
> I would strike with delight the harp of gold
> Which for me is reserved above,
> And sing — though its greatness can ne'er be told,
> Redeeming, dying love."[247]

---

[247] I have not been able to identify this poem or its author with certainly. One possible author however is Amey Scott, whose memoirs were published in 1840 [Mrs. Amey Scott, Memoirs (Lowell: E. A.
Rice and Co., 1840).] Written with dated entries like a journal, Mrs. Scott's book included occasional excerpts of hymns, among them one of Sarah's favorites: "O for a heart to praise my God." Scott's
memoir is more narrative and literary than Sarah's, but like hers, intersperses daily activities with religious reflections. Several poems by Scott are included in Memoirs, but not the poem Sarah included
here. It is possible she may have published individual poems in magazines or journals.

Aprail 9 Sabbeth

Went to church all of us and shut the house up.

April 11 Tuesday

Mr Reid went to new york. I took him to freehold came back and stoped to aunt margarets.

Aprail 12 Wednesday

Lizzie went to freehold to take Lizzie Applegate.

Aprail 14 friday

Nice day. Busy all day sewing. Mr Reid came home in the evening. I was very glad to see him. He had been gone since Tuesday.

Aprail 15 Saturday

Very busy cleaning my bedroom.

Aprail 16 Sabbeth

Went to church with Mr Reid. Herd a splendid sermon from the Rev Archibald Cobb from the text Lord what whilt thou have me to do. I was so much pleased with it. It was excellent. He spoke about not fetching the poor to church with us. I wish he would say more on that subject.

Aprail 17 Monday

A nice day. Lizzie washed & Mary Jane Appelgate helped her. When we sit down to dinner, Mr Reid said she was very nasty & she herd him and her feelings was so much hurt about it she cried herself most sick. She was in a tremble and would not eat any dinner, went home. I could not do any thing with her. I was very sorry to have her feelings so hurt.

Aprail 18 Tuesday

We all arose very early. Mr Reid went to new york in the six oclock train. I baked bread pies & cake in the fore noon and went to Tillies in the afternoon. Staid about five minutes and started for home. It was five oclock when I reached there. Stoped at Garrets store. Drove home very smart. Arived home before dark after sundown. Paid Mr Shepherd five dollars for Mr Shepherd and likewise five dollars to Mr Van cleft.

Aprail 19 Wednesday

A dull day. Lizzie went to englishtown & Kate Reid & Lizzie Appelgate came home with her. It rained when they came home.

Aprail 20 Thursday

All well. Very busy.

Aprail 23 [Sunday]

Nice day. The girls all went to church and Elwood & Jake Appelgate came home with them. They took them back in the evening.

Aprail 24 Monday

Lizzie went to freehold. I sewed on my black silk dress.

Aprail 25 Tuesday

Nice day. We washed in the morning & went to aunt margarets in the afternoon. I was worked almost sick. I worked very hard all day.

Aprail 29 Saturday

The girls went in the eve after Elwood and came home about half past ten.

Aprail 30 Sabbeth

A nice day. We could not go to church. Elwood wanted the black horse & buggy. We could not go without her. Con and Tillie and their five little ones came about ten oclock. We was very glad to see them. Had a nice time. Elwood went to Key port. Lizzie & Kate went home with Leander Jewell in the eve.

May 1 Monday

Nice day. Elwood came home about ten oclock. Lizzie & Florance went with him to freehold in the afternoon & went in to see the show of animals.[248]

May 2 Tuesday

Nice day. I cleaned the sitting room. I white washed the ceiling and was very tired at night. Lizzie & Florance helped me clean.

May 3 Wednesday

I was very busy baking and almost sick from the effects of house cleaning. Uncle bennie helped billie [249] plant corn and at the dinner table billie told me the old hog was sick. I amso worried about it. I do not know what to do if it dies.

---

[248] Though the *Monmouth Democrat* did not carry articles identifying this show, it did run an article noting that Barnum's circus was touring New Jersey, commenting that "as to the circus, so called, it unhappily has surroundings which are not at all commendable....Even the zoological accompaniment–the very animals, how wretched their short existence, so comfortless and unnatural." [May 4, 1871]

[249] Billie: a hired hand.

It will be a great looss for us. We have been scant of hogs for a great while and now had a prospect of plenty this year but God is so good my heart rejoices that God is always near and ready to help in every time of need and can be a refuge in every trial and so ready to forgive the vilest and chief of sinners. Tears blinds me almost when I think of his wonderful goodness & greatness & holiness to the children of men. Oh to be sheltered with such goodness and greatness and love. What can a soul want besides such a God of mercy.

I have been worked so very hard that I could not write. I was so very weak I could scarcely sit up and work work all day many times not even time to comb my head.

July 4 1871 [Tuesday]

Mr Reid was home and his brother Spafford made us a visit and took dinner. Had a nice time.

July 19 1871 [Wednesday]

Nice day. Went to the old church to attend the funeral of Joseph Denice.[250] He died very suden in Vermont and was brought on in the cars last night. We could not be seen to day. He died last sabbeth and, I was not so very much pleased with the sermon as I would have been if Mr Cobb had preached more to the young men to prepare in youth for a dying day to make it their first business to love & serve the saviour who loves them so much.

Nov 29 1871 [Wednesday]

Very busy baking and preparing for Thanks giving, and Mr Reid came in very unexpectedly. We was all glad to see him. I was all the week wishing he would come. A very cold day.

Nov 30 Thursday thanksgiving

A very cold morning. We expected company from hobocan [Hoboken] but they did not come. I have worked very hard all the week to have every thing nice for them. It is my birth day[251] and we have enjoyed it very much but it would have been a great comfort to have had our absent son and daughter with us. I had a nice pressent from Elwood of a half dozen silver forks. The nicest birth day pressent I have had.

Dec 1 friday 1871

Was a very cold morning. Very busy trying lard and cutting sauciges all day.[252] Florrance had a head ache all day. Very sick all night.

[250] Joseph Denise: probably the son of Garret and Virginia Denise.
[251] This was Sarah's 53rd birthday.
[252] Sausage and lard making were tasks which followed the slaughtering of hogs.

Dec 2 saturday

Very busy putting away lard and saturdays work for the sabbeth. Florance was sick up stairs and made me have extra work. Mr Smith and the Ridgeway machine man called and cleaned our sewing machine.

Dec 3 Sabbeth

I was almost worked sick and Florance was better. Lizie had a bad toothache. Elwood come home in the morning. Con & Tillie came with their little ones and took dinner. We spent a very pleasant day. Our dear ones all home and there never is an unkind word or look from any of us when we meet. No one is ever sent away with the slightest wound in their feelings, or any things to caus unkind feelings. I always do all I can to make them have a pleasant meeting. I never saw discord among my children but try to smothe evry path. They may walk a rough road but they will always remember that their home was made smothe as a mothers hand could make it.

Dec 4 Monday

Rainy and wet. Mr Reid went to New York in the early train. He would not let me get up and get his breckfast. He said I was so tired the night before he would get his own brackfast. Billie took him to the cars and then took Elwood to freehold after I had got the breckfast. Very busy all day. Lizzie helped me but her toung costs me many a tear. I wish I could go on and not care what is said to me. The trials of earth is very short. I wish I could take courage and bear all bravely knowing that there is a reward for all we bear for Jesus.

Dec 22 friday

A very cold day. Ground covered with snow. Myself and two young dauters one ten the other fourteen worked hard all day fixing for christmas baking bread and mince pies and a large splended fruit cake. All well done but beating the cake was the most tiresome job. Then we pick [pluck] a turkey for christmas dinner likewise two hens & was almost done when Mr Reid came home.[253] We was so busy fixing for him.

Dec 23 [Saturday]

A stormy day. We was a going to have a splendid slay ride but the storm commenced before we got ready to start. The children was very much disapointed about their ride.

Dec 24 [Sunday]

A splendid day. I was home from church and spent the [day] very pleasantly. In the evening Tillie came with her little children to spend christmas.

[253] This marks the end of William Reid's seasonal work in New York City for 1871.

home we was so busy fixing for him.

Dec 23
a stormy day we was a going to have
a splendid slay ride but the storm commenced
before we got ready to start. The children was
very much disappointed about their ride

Dec 24
a splendid day I was home from church
and spent the very pleasantly. in the evening
Tillie came with her Dec 25
little children to spend a very pleasant day
christmas Tillie and Con went home
in the afternoon with their little ones
after having a very nice time with them
we had a very glad time and a very nice
dinner which we all enjoyed;

Dec 26
a very dull day we all
went in the morning to englishtown.

Dec 27 wednesday
a blustery day Lizzie and
Florence Augusta went to see their cousin
Leander Jewell Married to their cousin Kate
Reid, Me and my husband have spent
the evening alone which we very seldom
do. I have been thinking that my dreams
of childhood have been realized in a great
many ways God has blessed me far more
than I ever deserved or could have expected.
I have had to work, but I am willing to work
I feel to night that the most of my life
has been sunshine and when dark clouds pre
vail they have had a silver lining; my
heart has always been the bright spot always
contented and hopeful and joyful God has
been so good to me More than I could tell

Dec 25 [Monday]

A very pleasant day. Tillie and Con went home in the afternoon with their little ones after having a very nice time with them. We had a very glad time and a very nice dinner which we all enjoyed.

Dec 26 [Tuesday]

A very dull day. We all went in the morning to englishtown.

Dec 27 Wednesday

A blustery day. Lizzie and Florance Agusta went to see their cousin Leander Jewell married to their cousin Kate Reid. Me and my husband have spent the evening alone which we very seldome do. I have been thinking that my dreams of childhood have been realized in a great many ways. God has blessed me far more than I ever deserved or could have expected. I have had to work, but I am willing to work. I feel to night that the most of my life has been sunshine and when dark clouds prevail they have had a silver lining. My heart has always been the bright spot always contented and hopeful and joyful. God has been so good to me more than I could ask.

Jan 23 Tuesday [1872]

Done all the morning work and washed got dinner and worked until five minutes of four and did not wash the dinner dishes and my children did not like it that I did not wash the dinner dishes. My heart is so much torn by there unkindness and unkind words. I hope no mother will fetch their children up so tenderly as I have done and for so little thanks. I wash all day and they was not willing that I should rest when I was so tired my wrists pained me and my side pained and was swelled all night and all the next day. Lizzie & Florance is not willing to help with the work after school. I dare not let their father know how they talk to me.

1873

Had the rheumatism not able to work. Worked all day until three oclock at house work and then sit down to flora dress. Worke until four ——

Dec 26 [1873? Friday]

A stormy day. Done all I could on Lizzies blue empress cloth dress and oh how much unkindness I have borne from her to day. Called me a lior and said she had have so much of my impudence. The tears she has made me shed. I could not keep from crying to night. May God forgive her for her treatment of me. It is the truth. You tell what is not so.[254]

Sarah T Reid

[254] The final two brief sentences of the diary are in a different hand writing. The diary stops here.

ADDENDUM

Ye bells throughout through out the land

Toll toll toll, on evry hand on every hand
Ye bells ye bells thru out the land
      Ye bells thro-out the land
Our noble leader noble head in
        in his glory lies; The damp of death
The damp of death uppon his sealed eyes
A martyr true, a martyr true to liberty he dies
Toll toll toll, in every hand on evry hand
Ye bells thro out the land thro out the land
      Toll toll toll.

Weep weep weep on every hand
  on every hand
Ye heroes heroes of the land
  ye heroes of the land
Our chieftain chieftain dead
  Great God and can it be!
Alas how brief Alas how bried is our
  Mortallity
Our Father help, O help and bless to us
this agony! Weep weep weep on every
hand on every hand! Ye heroes
heroes in the land Weep weep weep

Mourn mourn mourn on every hand
  on every hand
Ye patriots of the land
  Ye patriots of the land!
  No more no more his honest face will
  greet the sun
his day his day this day is finished and
  his labor done.
A crown of Glory crown of Glory sits
  his brow upon.
Mourn mourn mourn on every hand
  on every hand Ye patriots patriots
    in the land,
  Mourn mourn mourn[255]

---

[255] Sarah has transcribed the Lincoln elegy here.

[in a childlike hand]   West Freehold Dec 18th 1869

My Dear Lidie

 You must excuse me for not writing sooner, Father Mother and Brother to was to Lizzie Perine weding last thurday had a splendid time her husband made her a presant of a gold wach and chaine   [in Sarah's hand] and a silver ice pitcher a cake basket silver butter dish two silver cream pitcher one sugar bowl one dozen tea spoons and some smaller articles I have my new dress almost done, we have two pink tea roses out to day, we are invited out to spend christmas[256]

---

[256]This letter refers to the wedding of Lizzie Perrine and James J. Taylor, noted in Sarah's entry for December 9, 1869.

Index

Bibliography

Alexander, Archibald D.D. *Thoughts on Religious Experience*. Philadelphia: Presbyterian Board of Publication, 1844.

Atlas of Monmouth County, New Jersey. New York: Beers, Comstock and Cline, 1873.

Brown, Arthur Judson. *One Hundred Years*. New York: Fleming H. Revell Co., 1934.

Brown, James S. *Manalapan in Three Centuries*. Manalapan: Township of Manalapan, 1991.

Bunkers, Suzanne L. and Cynthia A. Huff. *Inscribing the Daily: Critical Essays on Women's Diaries*. Amherst: University of Massachusetts Press, 1996.

Burstyn, Joan N., ed. *Past and Promise Lives of New Jersey Women*. Syracuse: Syracuse University Press, 1997.

Clark, Clifford Edward, Jr. *The American Family Home: 1800-1960*. Chapel Hill: University of North Carolina Press, 1986,

Cowan, Ruth Schwartz. *More Work for Mother: The Ironies of Household Technology from the Open Hearth to the Microwave*. New York: Basic Books, 1983.

Doddridge, Philip, D.D., *The Rise and Progress of Religion in the Soul illustrated in a course of serious and practical addresses suited to persons of every character and circumstance*. Philadelphia: Presbyterian Board of Publication, 1843. First published in 1744.

Ellis, Franklin. *History of Monmouth County*. Philadelphia: 1885. Reprint facsimile, 1974.

Gordon, Larry and Anthony G. Barrand, eds., *Northern Harmony*. Plainfield, VT: Northern Harmony Publishing Co., 1998.

Greeley, Horace, *What I Know of Farming: A Series of Brief and Plain Expositions* . New York: G. W. Carleton & Co., 1871.

Griffin, William L. *150 Years of Ministry, 1838-1988: The First Presbyterian Church of Freehold, New Jersey*. No date. Limited edition, 1989.

Hamilton, James, D.D. *The Mount of Olives; and other lectures on prayer*. New York: R. Carter, 1846.

Hymnal, Ordered by the General Assembly. Philadelphia: Presbyterian Board of Publication, 1867.

Kagle, Steven E. *American Diary Literature, 1620-1799*. Boston: Twayne Publishers, 1979.

MacDonald, James M. D.D. *My Father's House; or, The Heaven of the Bible*. New York: Charles Scribner, 1856.

Medical Society of New Jersey. *Transactions*, 1882.

Missionary Herald, 1869-1870-1871.

Monmouth County Directory for 1875. Freehold, 1875.

Monmouth Democrat, 1869-1872.

Monmouth Democrat, *Almanac for the year 1871*.

Presbyterian Synod of New Jersey. *Minutes of the Synod of New Jersey for the year ending October 1869*. New Brunswick, 1869.

Princeton Theological Seminary. *Biographical Catalogue*. Princeton: Theological Seminary of the Presbyterian Church, 1933.

Psalms and Hymns, Adapted to Social, Private, and Public Worship in the Presbyterian Church. Philadelphia: Presbyterian Board of Publication, 1843.

Schmidt, Hubert G. *Agriculture in New Jersey: A Three-Hundred- Year History*. New Brunswick: Rutgers University Press, 1973.

Strasser, Susan. *Never Done: A History of American Housework*. New York: Pantheon Books, 1982.

Symmes, Rev. Frank R. *History of the Old Tennent Church*. Cranbury: George W. Burroughs, 1904.

United States, Manuscript Census of Monmouth County, New Jersey, 1870.

Weintraub, Jeff and Krishan Kumar. *Public and Private in Thought and Practice*. Chicago: University of Chicago Press, 1997.

Western Theological Seminary. *Historical and Biographical Catalogue*. Allegheny, PA: The Seminary, 1885.

Wilson, Harold F. *The Jersey Shore: A Social and Economic History of the Counties of Atlantic, Cape May, Monmouth and Ocean*. New York: Lewis Historical Publishing Co., 1953.

Vecoli, Rudolph J. *The People of New Jersey*. Princeton: D. Van Nostrand Co., 1965.